WITHDRAWN
From the
Dean B. Ellis Library
Arkansas State University

DEAN B ELLIS LIBRARY

Columbia University

Contributions to Education

Teachers College Series

No. 175

AMS PRESS
NEW YORK

MEASURING EFFICIENCY IN SUPERVISION AND TEACHING

BY

LELAH MAE CRABBS, Ph.D.

Teachers College, Columbia University
Contributions to Education, No. 175

Published by
Teachers College, Columbia University
New York City
1925

Library of Congress Cataloging in Publication Data

Crabbs, Lelah Mae, 1885-
  Measuring efficiency in supervision and teaching.

  Reprint of the 1925 ed., issued in series: Teachers College, Columbia University. Contributions to education, no. 175.
  Originally presented as the author's thesis, Columbia.
  Bibliography: p.
  1. Teachers, Rating of. 2. Mental tests. I. Title II. Series: Columbia University. Teachers College. Contributions to education, no. 175.
LB2838.C67 1972   372.11'44   73-176676
ISBN 0-404-55175-0

Reprinted by Special Arrangement with Teachers College Press, New York, New York

From the edition of 1925, New York
First AMS edition published in 1972
Manufactured in the United States

AMS PRESS, INC.
NEW YORK, N. Y. 10003

PREFATORY NOTE

It is my pleasure to make grateful acknowledgments to the following members of my Dissertation Committee, who supervised the preparation of this study: Professor M. B. Hillegas, Professor Wm. H. Kilpatrick, Professor Wm. A. McCall, and Professor A. I. Gates, of Teachers College.

Also, I wish to record my gratitude to Superintendent Thomas Gordon Bennett who supervised the administration, scoring and checking of all the tests given in Queen Anne's County, Maryland. It has not been my pleasure to find a more generous professional attitude than that manifested by him and his staff.

Miss Roxanna Steele kindly loaned the data for the Steele-Herring Professional Knowledge Test.

L. M. C.

CONTENTS

PART ONE—MEASURING SUPERVISION

CHAP.   PAGE

I. PROGRAM OF MEASUREMENT 1
   1. The Problem 1
   2. Statement of Conditions 2
   3. Tests and Testing Procedure 3

II. PROGRAM OF SUPERVISION 6
   1. Purpose of the School in Having This Program 6
   2. Reporting General Results 6
   3. Reporting Individual School, Class and Pupil Status . . . 11
   4. Other Features of the Supervision Program 13
   5. Suggested Improvements in Procedure 18

III. EVALUATION OF THE SUPERVISION 20

PART TWO—MEASURING TEACHING

IV. STAGES IN THE EVOLUTION OF METHODS 27
   1. General Impression Method 27
   2. Score Card Method 28
   3. Objective Measurement Method 30

V. COMPUTATION OF EFFICIENCY MEASURES FOR EACH TEACHER 32
   1. Source and Nature of Data for the Computations 32
   2. Computation of Teacher Efficiency Measures in Each Subject 33
   3. Computation of a Composite Measure of the Teacher's Efficiency 38

VI. CORRELATION BETWEEN OBJECTIVE EFFICIENCY MEASURES . . . 41
   1. To What Extent is a Teacher's Efficiency in Teaching Reading an Index of His Efficiency in Teaching Other Subjects? 41
   2. To What Extent is a Teacher's Efficiency in Teaching Arithmetic an Index of His Efficiency in Teaching Other Subjects? 46
   3. To What Extent is a Teacher's Efficiency in Teaching Spelling an Index of His Efficiency in Teaching Other Subjects? 47
   4. To What Extent is a Teacher's Efficiency in Teaching Composition an Index of His Efficiency in Teaching Other Subjects? 48

CONTENTS

CHAP.   PAGE

    5. To What Extent is a Teacher's Efficiency in Teaching Penmanship an Index of His Efficiency in Teaching Other Subjects? 50
    6. Can One Predict a Teacher's Ability to Teach a Narrow Skill from Knowledge of His Ability to Teach Another Narrow Skill Better Than from Knowledge of His Ability to Teach a Less Narrow Skill—and Vice Versa? 51

VII. CORRELATION BETWEEN EFFICIENCY MEASURES AND SUPERVISORS' ESTIMATES 54
    1. To What Extent is a Supervisor Able to Judge Teachers' Efficiency in Teaching Reading? 54
    2. What is the Correlation Between Ability to Teach Skills and Estimated Ability to Teach Everything Except Character? 56
    3. What is the Correlation Between Ability to Teach Skills and Estimated Ability to Build Character? 57
    4. What is the Correlation Between Ability to Teach Skills and Estimated Ability to Teach in General? 57
    5. What are the Intercorrelations Between Estimates of Teachers' Ability to Teach Reading, to Teach Everything Except Character, and to Build Character? 58
    6. What is the Estimate of Competent Judges as to the Size and Direction of Certain Efficiency Correlations Already Reported? 60
    7. To What Extent is Professional Knowledge an Index of Teaching Efficiency? 64

VIII. CRITICISMS OF THE VALIDITY OF THE TEACHING-EFFICIENCY FORMULA 67
    1. Does the Type of School Give a Special Advantage or Handicap to the Teacher? 67
    2. Does Initial IQ of the Class Affect the Validity of the Formula for the Measurement of Teaching Efficiency? ... 71
    3. Does the Initial AR of the Class Affect the Validity of the Formula for Measuring Teaching Efficiency? 81
    4. Does the Formula for the Measurement of Teaching Efficiency Yield a Valid Measure of General Teaching Efficiency? 86

PART THREE

IX. SUMMARY AND CONCLUSIONS 91

TABLES

CHAP.		PAGE
I.	Total Subject Units and Total Subject Unit Gains Found as a Result of the Two Measurement Programs, October 1922 and October 1923	23
II.	Computation of Efficiency Measures for a Teacher	34
III.	Rho's Between Supervisors' Rankings of Teachers' Ability to Teach (1) Comprehension in Reading, (2) Everything except Character, and (3) Character	59
IV.	Various Intercorrelations between Teaching Efficiency Measures and Supervisory Rankings of Teacher Efficiency, together with Estimates of What These Correlations Are	61
V.	Distribution of Mean AR Changes for Each Class for Each Subject and for Each Type of School, and the Total for All Types	68
VI.	Correlations between Pupil IQ and Pupil RAR Gain in One-, Two- and Three-room Rural Schools	74

DIAGRAMS

I.	A Comparison of the Attainment of the Various Grades in October 1922 (black bar) and the Standard Norm for Each Grade in October (white bar) and for the Woody-McCall Mixed Fundamentals in Arithmetic in June (shaded bar)	8
II.	Frequency Distribution of Crude Scores on the National Intelligence Test, Scale A, Form I, for Each Grade in October. The Heavy Vertical Bars Indicate the 25 Percentile and the 75 Percentile for Each Grade	10
III.	The Upper Diagram Shows Which Pupils Fell Above, Below and in the Normal (90–110) IQ Group. The Lower Diagram Shows Which Pupils Fell Below and Which Exceeded the Standard Norm 140. These Data Are Based on Subject Ages and Mental Ages	12
IV.	Showing the Pupils in a Class Ranked in Intelligence on the Basis of Test Results (black) and According to the Teacher's Judgment (white). Thus, the Pupil Ranked 29 on Test Results Was Ranked 8 by the Teacher	16
V.	Showing the Pupils in a Class Ranked in Achievement in Reading on the Basis of the Test Results (black) and According to the Teacher's Judgment (white). Thus, the Pupil Ranked 10 on the Test Results Was Ranked 18 by the Teacher	17
VI.	Comparison of the Achievement in Reading and Arithmetic by the Various Grades for October 1922 and October 1923, with the Standard Norm	25

PART ONE

MEASURING SUPERVISION

CHAPTER I

PROGRAM OF MEASUREMENT

THE PROBLEM

This study is concerned with measurement in the field of supervision and teaching in the elementary school. It aims:
I. To evolve a technique of supervision based on measurement;
II. To evolve a technique of measuring the efficiency of this supervision;
III. To apply the AR technique of measuring the efficiency of teaching in both rural and urban school systems and to study certain problems that arise in the treatment of the data. A list of these problems follows:

1. To what extent is a teacher's efficiency in teaching reading an index of his efficiency in teaching other subjects?
2. To what extent is a teacher's efficiency in teaching arithmetic an index of his efficiency in teaching other subjects?
3. To what extent is a teacher's efficiency in teaching spelling an index of his efficiency in teaching other subjects?
4. To what extent is a teacher's efficiency in teaching composition an index of his efficiency in teaching other subjects?
5. To what extent is a teacher's efficiency in teaching penmanship an index of his efficiency in teaching other subjects?
6. Can one predict a teacher's ability to teach a narrow skill from knowledge of his ability to teach another narrow skill better than from knowledge of his ability to teach a less narrow skill—and vice versa?
7. To what extent is a supervisor able to judge teachers' efficiency in teaching reading?
8. What is the correlation between ability to teach skills and estimated ability to teach everything except character?

2   EFFICIENCY IN SUPERVISION AND TEACHING

9. What is the correlation between ability to teach skills and estimated ability to build character?

10. What is the correlation between ability to teach skills and estimated ability to teach in general?

11. What are the intercorrelations between estimates of teachers' ability to teach reading, to teach everything except character, and to build character?

12. What is the estimate of competent judges as to the size and direction of the foregoing efficiency correlations?

13. To what extent is professional knowledge an index of teaching efficiency?

14. Does the type of school give a special advantage or handicap to the teacher?

15. Does the initial IQ of the class affect the validity of the formula for the measurement of teaching efficiency?

16. Does the initial AR of the class affect the validity of the formula for measuring teaching efficiency?

17. Does the formula for the measurement of teaching efficiency yield a valid measure of general teaching efficiency?

STATEMENT OF CONDITIONS

1. The urban situation alone enters into the supervision phase of this program.

2. The district is wholly a residential town of approximately 10,000 population.

3. In financial resources, as shown in the assessed wealth per inhabitant of $1,400, the town stands sixth in a group of eleven similar districts. The assessed wealth per pupil living in the district is $6,077, which gives it the rank of seventh in this respect. The state average is $6,090. The town's assessed wealth consists largely of homes. It has no industries or business properties, which contribute heavily to the evaluation in large cities. This statement calls attention to the reason why the town ranks fourth highest in the list of eleven districts in amount raised for schools per capita.

4. The cost of education per pupil enrolled is $100.53, in which respect the town ranks seventh in this group of districts. The state average is $73.35.

5. Though the town appears as an approximate average of the districts with which it is compared in these various respects, these

PROGRAM OF MEASUREMENT

districts are between thirty-five and forty per cent. higher than the state average.

6. At the time of this study the town had seven schools, a teaching staff of eighty-seven, and a registration of over two thousand pupils. Over five hundred of these were high school pupils, and about three hundred and fifty were enrolled in a grammar school including all seventh and eighth grades in the system.

7. The records of approximately eleven hundred pupils form the basis for the problems studied in relation to the urban situation.

8. The town had had no previous systematic testing program, though unorganized measuring in various phases of school work had been carried on during the preceding two years.

9. The attitude of the superintendent and the principals of schools was scientific from the beginning and throughout the program. They were willing and anxious to face the results of the program, to acknowledge at all times the weak spots in their system and to consider what might be done to bring about needed change. This coöperation rendered feasible a much more thorough survey and study of conditions, and the use of more complete diagnostic and remedial measures than would have been possible otherwise.

10. Virtually all teachers were graduates of normal schools within the state, but few had had additional training.

11. The teachers were aided in their work by the supervision of a superintendent, three special supervisors of music, art and physical education respectively, a full-time principal in each school, and a part-time director of measurement.

12. Parent-teachers associations were active, showing an interest in all school matters that affected the education of the town's children.

TESTS AND TESTING PROCEDURE

The tests used in the urban situation were:

1. *Intelligence Tests:* National Intelligence Test: Scale A—Form I. Herring Revision of the Binet-Simon Tests: Form A.

2. *Educational Tests:* Thorndike-McCall Reading Scale: Forms 4 and 5. Woody-McCall Mixed Fundamentals: Forms 1 and 2. Morrison-McCall Spelling Scale: Lists 1 and 2. Nassau County Supplement to the Hillegas Composition Scale. Gettysburg Edition of the Ayres Penmanship Scale.

The following is an outline of the procedure used in the testing program:

1. Two days a week throughout the year were spent by the writer as director of measurement in the school system.

2. Grades three to eight inclusive formed the unit for the first year's study for the following reasons: (*a*) It was obviously impracticable for one person without clerical aid to attempt a more extensive program. (*b*) More and better standardized tests were available for this period than for the primary and high school periods.

3. The first measurement program was conducted in October 1922. It included one form of each of the tests listed above, with the exception of the Herring individual intelligence examination. This was administered in the spring of the school year to a selected group of children for specific reasons, which will be explained in the next chapter.

4. All tests were administered by the director with the incidental assistance of the classroom teacher. The standardized procedure for administering tests was employed.

5. The tests were scored by the teachers under the supervision of the director. The scoring was done in accordance with the standardized procedure.

6. Later the tests were checked and the results tabulated and graphed by the director.

7. Then there followed a series of general teachers' meetings, group teachers' meetings, principals' meetings, and parent-teacher association meetings which will be described in the next chapter.

8. In October, 1923, the measurement program was repeated with a different but duplicate form of each of the educational tests. These tests were administered, scored and tabulated by a group of graduate students in measurement and elementary education in Teachers College, who had been carefully trained and were closely supervised by the director. The National Intelligence Test was given to only those pupils for whom a record had not been secured during the previous year.

9. The crude scores on the National Intelligence, Herring, Thorndike-McCall, Woody-McCall, Morrison-McCall, Nassau and Ayres Tests were converted into group mental age, individual mental age, reading age, arithmetic age, spelling age, composition age, and penmanship age respectively, according to tables accom-

panying these tests, or according to tables constructed in accordance with principles discussed in McCall's *How to Measure in Education,* Chapter II.[1]*

10. Intelligence Quotient, Reading Quotient, and the other Subject Quotients were computed by dividing the respective mental age or subject age by the chronological age of the pupils and multiplying by one hundred.

11. Reading Accomplishment Ratio and the other Subject Ratios were computed by dividing the respective ages for each pupil by his mental age and then multiplying by one hundred.

* Throughout this study numbers in brackets refer to numbered references in the Bibliography, page 98.

CHAPTER II

PROGRAM OF SUPERVISION

THE PURPOSE OF THE SCHOOL IN HAVING THIS PROGRAM

The testing program was not instituted because the town was in such bad condition educationally that drastic remedial measures were deemed necessary. Conventional opinion would probably have ranked the district among the best of our public school systems. It must simply be considered among the pioneers in a movement that has spread rapidly and far during the last few years. The staff was working earnestly to secure the educational results that they thought desirable, but they recognized the fact that their judgments were largely guesses and hence wished to make use of some of the objective measures then available.

Initial steps had been taken to secure, from the principals of the schools, questions that they wished to have answered by data from the measurements. These questions furnished the guide for the first steps in the program. This statement offers the keynote to the director's procedure throughout the supervision phase of the study. Rarely were facts and information given to superintendent, principals or teachers until questions from them called for answers.

The questions that initiated this program were: What kind of mental material have we with which to work? How do the results of our teaching compare with standard norms? Within our system, where is our strength—and our weakness? How can we improve our situation?

REPORTING GENERAL RESULTS

The manner in which general results of the first measurement program were reported to the teaching staff is shown in Diagram 1. Though only grades three to eight inclusive were measured, all teachers, principals and special supervisors of elementary schools were requested to be present at a general meeting called by the

PROGRAM OF SUPERVISION

superintendent for the purpose of reporting and discussing results.

The procedure used by the director at this first general meeting was as follows:

1. To state and answer the first three questions that had been asked by the superintendent and principals of the schools at a previous meeting with them. The questions were: What kind of mental material have we with which to work? How do the results of our teaching compare with standard norms? Within our system, where is our strength—and our weakness?

2. To secure as much as possible of the interpretation of results from the group present.

3. To secure a new set of questions that would serve as a guide to further steps in the program.

4. To secure from the teachers, if possible, a repetition of question four—How can we improve our situation?—and to let this serve as the basis for a second general meeting.

5. To introduce the problem of classification. No question from the group had initiated this phase of the program, but since the data showed that it needed attention in their situation, it was thought desirable to stimulate consciousness of the existence of the problem.

It was sincerely hoped that this meeting would secure the same degree of interest and desire to coöperate from the teachers that had been shown from the beginning by the principals and the superintendent. A brief report of the most significant features of this meeting follows:

A deliberate effort was made to strip the report of all technical language, the attempt to acquaint the staff with even the simplest technical terms of the field being left until after the value of the program had been demonstrated. For similar reasons the bar diagram, the simplest to interpret, was used to show the norm in each phase of the program and the relative achievement in their own situation. Large graphs eighteen by twenty-four inches, like those shown in Diagram 1, which could be seen easily by all in the room, were used to show the staff the town's status in intelligence and in each of the educational subjects measured.

After a brief preliminary introduction, which included a statement of the purposes of the measurement program, an explanation of the meaning of the series of bars in Diagram 1 was given. It was pointed out that the white bar in each instance showed the

8   EFFICIENCY IN SUPERVISION AND TEACHING

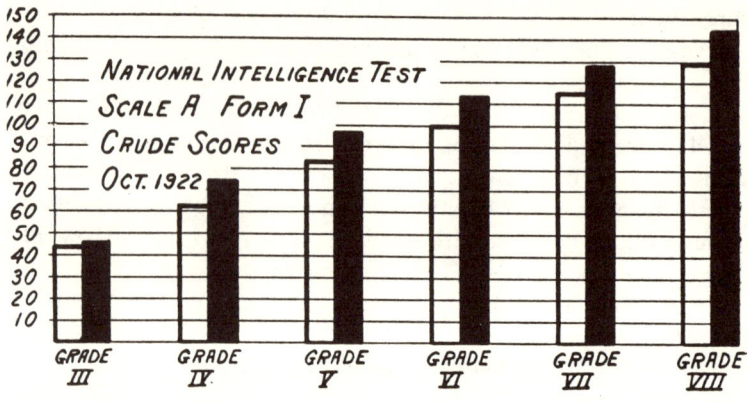
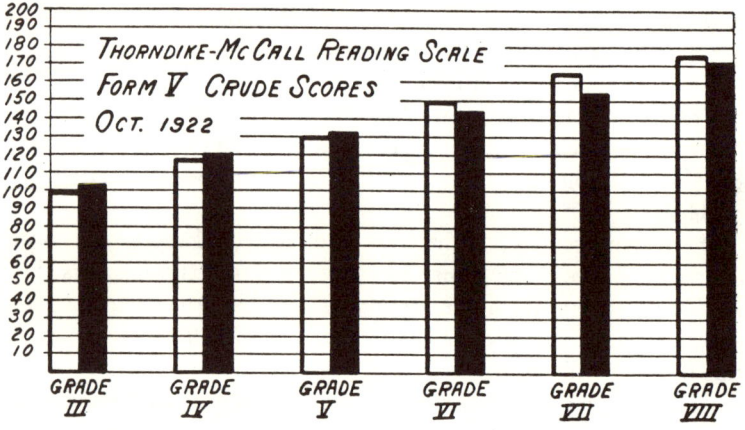
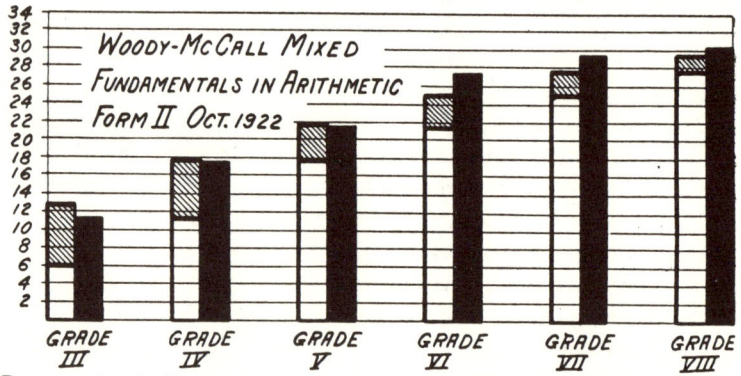

DIAGRAM 1. A COMPARISON OF THE ATTAINMENT OF THE VARIOUS GRADES IN OCTOBER 1922 (BLACK BAR) AND THE STANDARD NORM FOR EACH GRADE IN OCTOBER (WHITE BAR) AND FOR THE WOODY-MCCALL MIXED FUNDAMENTALS IN ARITHMETIC IN JUNE (SHADED BAR).

norm for the particular grade in a particular subject, while the black bar indicated the system's relative standing in each respect.

A period of inspection and discussion of the diagrams came next. Some of the more important points claiming attention follow:

1. That the pupils were shown to have better than average intelligence.
2. That, though satisfying, this higher intelligence level added a responsibility for the teaching staff. The pupils in each grade should also show better than average achievement in the school skills in which they had been measured.
3. That, in reading for comprehension, the third, fourth and fifth grades were achieving a little better than the standard norm, while the sixth, seventh and eighth grades were accomplishing much less than should be expected of them according to the standard norm.
4. That the staff had set their standard of comparison in teaching with other school systems containing pupils with lower average intelligence owing to the influence of a large foreign element in these communities.
5. That, in the fundamental processes in arithmetic, all grades were attaining, not only the grade norm, but an ability a year in advance of the norms.
6. That, two years earlier, the system had been measured in the fundamental processes of arithmetic and that they had at that time been found to be far behind the norm. Increased attention to the subject, more time and other factors had brought about the desired change.

Similar diagrams were shown for the other subjects and were briefly considered in the same manner.

A second series of diagrams for each phase of the program, like Diagram 2, was shown next. These were used to introduce the classification problem in general and to stimulate the staff to some consideration of its importance in their own system.

A brief explanation of these frequency distributions for each group showed that each small rectangle represented one child and that the two perpendicular lines dividing the distributions into three sections showed approximately the lowest twenty-five per cent., the middle fifty per cent., and the upper twenty-five per cent. of the pupils in each grade.

10 EFFICIENCY IN SUPERVISION AND TEACHING

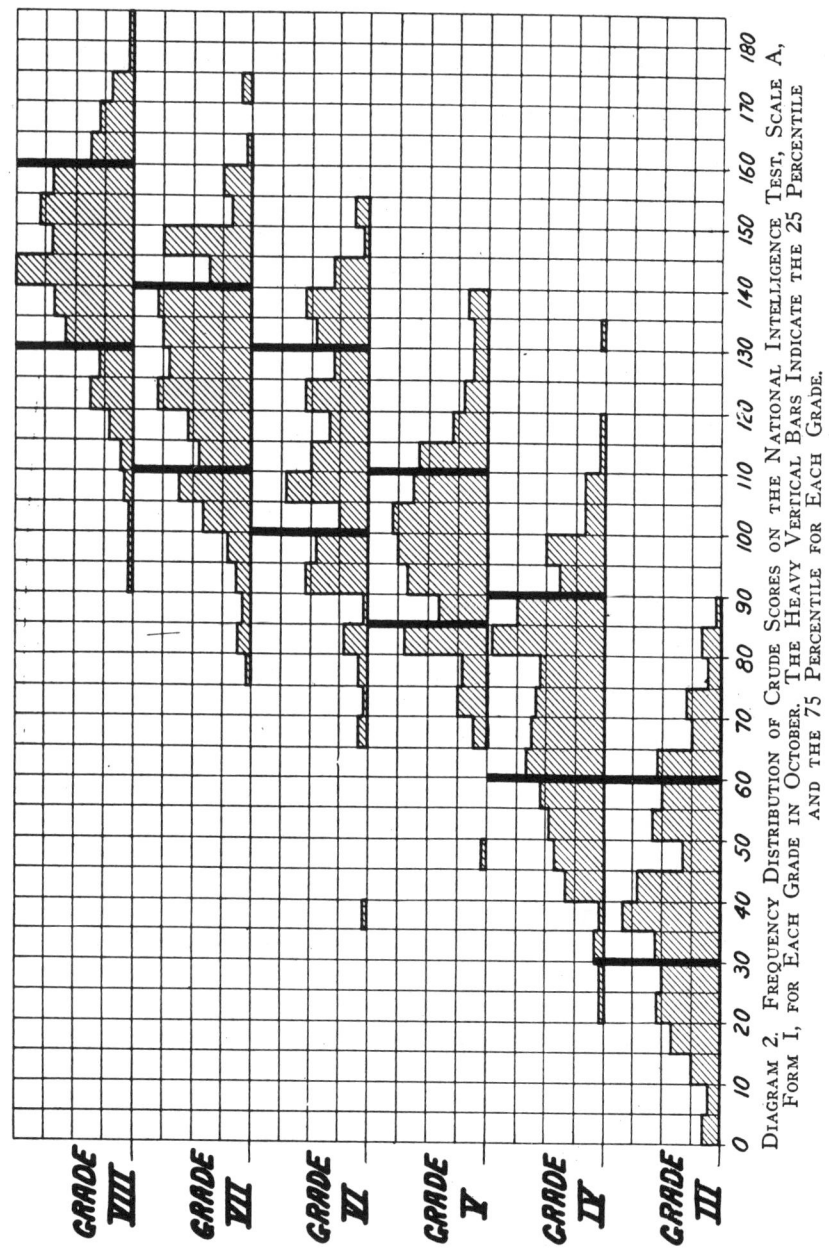

Diagram 2. Frequency Distribution of Crude Scores on the National Intelligence Test, Scale A, Form I, for Each Grade in October. The Heavy Vertical Bars Indicate the 25 Percentile and the 75 Percentile for Each Grade.

PROGRAM OF SUPERVISION

Some of the more important points brought out in connection with the interpretation of these diagrams follow:

1. That there was a wide range of ability in each grade.
2. That, according to test results, one pupil in the fourth grade possessed an ability level falling within the middle fifty per cent of the pupils in the eighth grade.
3. That one of the main uses of the group test was to focus attention for individual study on the too greatly retarded or too greatly accelerated pupil.

REPORTING INDIVIDUAL SCHOOL, CLASS AND PUPIL STATUS

Some of the principals thought it possible that one or two schools might be responsible for lowering the status of the entire system in a particular subject. It was in an effort to answer this question that diagrams similar to those shown in Diagram 1 were made in which each school was given a key color to distinguish it from the others. The relative position of each school in intelligence and in achievement in each of the school subjects measured was then graphed and each school was shown its position in the group. The precaution to protect each school's particular record, however, proved of little avail. The school that showed the lowest accomplishment in comparison with its intelligence rank was the first to announce the fact and ask for help.

The professional attitude in this school was excellent. The staff began at once a program of self study that was admirable. The principal and some members of the school staff visited, not schools in their own district this time, but schools that represented the best in the educational thought of today. They bought other tests and learned to measure in order to be sure that they really were improving. They held occasional extra meetings among themselves, discussing methods, new devices, etc.

They had prided themselves upon being the only school in the system using the project method and having freer discipline, but were willing to be shown that what they really had was just the reverse in method and that their freedom was almost pure license. These two factors alone might account for their lower achievement.

All individual class and pupil records were reported at staff meetings held at each school. General tendencies were indicated,

12 EFFICIENCY IN SUPERVISION AND TEACHING

but the emphasis at each of these meetings was placed upon the particular school's problems.

Crude scores had been used to report general results for two reasons. First, because it is usually conceded that, for a general view of the field, crude scores give as good picture of conditions as ages do, and second, because it was possible in this way to get the report before the group much earlier than it could have been presented otherwise.

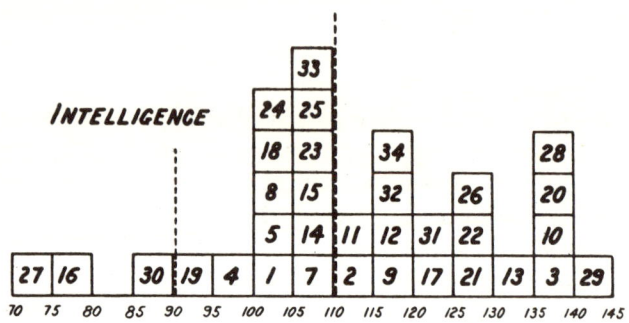

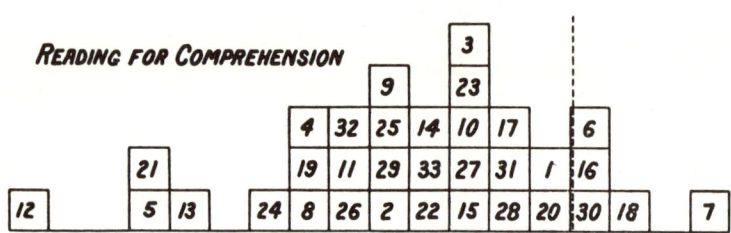

DIAGRAM 3. THE UPPER DIAGRAM SHOWS WHICH PUPILS FELL ABOVE, BELOW, AND IN THE NORMAL (90-110) IQ GROUP. THE LOWER DIAGRAM SHOWS WHICH PUPILS FELL BELOW AND WHICH EXCEEDED THE STANDARD NORM 140. THESE DATA ARE BASED ON SUBJECT AGES AND MENTAL AGES.

At the various school meetings an effort was made to secure from the teachers questions that they wished to have answered. These followed the general trend of the questions that had been asked by the principals at the general meeting. They were: What is the quality of the mental material with which I have to work? How does my class compare with the norm in achievement in the various school subjects? etc.

Diagram 3 shows the manner in which these questions were

answered. Mental age, reading age, arithmetic age, etc., formed the units used. The two perpendicular lines in this diagram mark off the group having average intelligence as shown by the test results, also the group below and the group above average in achievement. The numbers are code numbers for each pupil in the class.

The same type of diagram was used for reporting each subject, with the exception that only one perpendicular line was drawn to show the standard norm for the particular grade. All above the line were above the norm and all below the line were below the norm.

Diagrams such as those shown in Herring and Wilner's *Manual for Measuring a School* [2] were also used to portray individual class and individual pupil status.

OTHER FEATURES OF THE SUPERVISION PROGRAM

1. *Reclassification.* No attempt will be made to report thoroughly on the procedure used in dealing with the classification problem in this situation. The results pictured conditions that are typical of most of our public school systems over the country, and the usual steps were followed in an attempt to improve these conditions.

Pupils falling into the upper and lower twenty-five per cent. of the frequency distribution for each class, as shown in Diagram 2, received individual attention first. Where wide disagreement occurred between the test results and the teacher's judgment, an individual intelligence test was given, in order to have a second check on the child's general ability to achieve.

The state law stipulated that each board of education in the state should ascertain what children, if any, there were in the public schools who were three years or more below normal. In each school district where there were ten or more such children, a special class or classes were to be established for their instruction. No class, however, was to contain more than fifteen children. Therefore, emphasis was given first to the lower end of the curve, in order to find the particular pupils who would make up the group for special classes, should it be decided later that these could be formed.

Extra promotions were given to many pupils falling among the upper twenty-five per cent. Caution was taken here to consider all factors that enter into extra progress (such as physical condition, stage of maturity, social habits, etc.). Due to this careful study of each individual case, all extra promotions, at last reports, had proved successful.

2. *Board of Education Meetings.* By request, the director appeared before the Board of Education to give occasional reports of progress in the various phases of the program. The diagrams that had been presented at the general teachers' meetings were used again to give results of the measurement program. Every effort was made to secure the coöperation and interest of the members of the board by informing them of the various phases of the program and its place in their educational system. Careful note was taken of all questions asked by any of the members. It was some of these questions that initiated several supervisory techniques in this field.

3. *Parent-Teachers' Association Meetings.* Talks on measurement in general, its aims, particular values to a school system, to teachers, to the pupils, to parents, etc., were given at a general parent-teachers' association meeting and at meetings of most of the individual parent-teachers' associations. Ample opportunity was given to the parents to ask questions and to discuss school problems in this field. Definite attempts were made to bring them into closer association with the work. The same series of large graphs that was used at the teachers' meetings and the board meetings was used again at these meetings. All were informed as simply as possible of the aims and hopes of the measurement program. The results of various phases of the program were reported as the plans progressed.

4. *Parent Interviews.* A technique for conducting parent interviews is in the early stages of development. It was believed in the beginning that at least three different types of interview would be necessary for meeting the needs of the program, but after the first few had taken place it was observed that all seemed to center around a common core of procedure. In time it is probable that a very helpful technique can be evolved that will win for the workers in this field the coöperation of most parents. With few exceptions parents wish for their children the best that can be given to them. They also prefer to have them experience success rather than failure in whatever they attempt to accomplish. If some method can be found by which they can be convinced that an effort is being made to bring about the success and happiness

of their children, the aid rather than the opposition of a very important factor in the degree of success of attempts in this field will have been gained.

5. *Training Teachers to Build Better Types of Examination.* During the initial survey, several teachers had remarked that if the reading test used represented the kind of reading that was most desirable they would teach that kind. This suggested that more thoughtful testing of the children by the teachers for definite educational values might prove to be a very important factor in bringing about desired changes in teaching.

An inspection of the examinations being given by the teachers showed that very generally they were testing for the facts of a subject rather than for power to use these facts or for gain in power to think in a variety of ways with the materials of each subject. Some of the more able and interested teachers formed a group for the purpose of studying the newer types of examination and received aid in the construction of these for use in their own classes.

6. *Securing Interest on the Part of the Teachers in the Measurement Program.* Diagrams 4 and 5 illustrate one means that was used to secure consciousness on the part of the teachers of the possible aid which they might receive from concrete measurement in making judgments of children in their classes. The black circles in Diagram 4 show the pupils of one class ranked in order of the amount of intelligence possessed by each according to test results. The white circles indicate the rank given to each pupil in the class by the teacher according to her judgment of the amount of intelligence possessed by each. Diagram 5 tells the same story for the pupils' achievement in reading. A comparison of the two diagrams shows that this teacher could more accurately judge pupils in their actual achievement in reading in comparison with test results than in the amount of intelligence possessed by them. This same tendency was shown by similar diagrams made for each class in the system.

Aside from showing interesting general tendencies, these diagrams point out for the teacher the pupils over-rated and those under-rated by her in comparison with the rating given by the test, and focus attention for individual study. Care was taken to warn the teacher against accepting the test results as final. In some cases it might be possible that her judgment was truer than the test as a measure of the child's ability or achievement. In other

16 EFFICIENCY IN SUPERVISION AND TEACHING

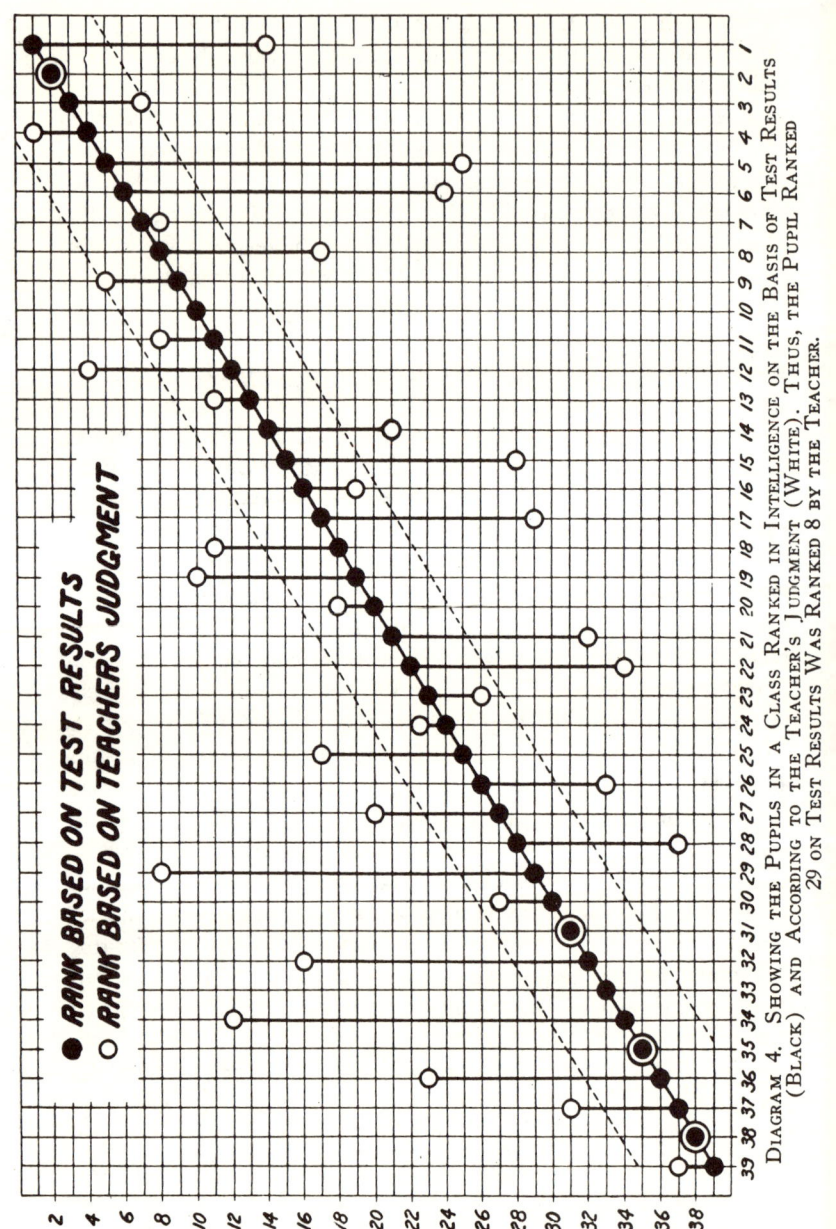

DIAGRAM 4. SHOWING THE PUPILS IN A CLASS RANKED IN INTELLIGENCE ON THE BASIS OF TEST RESULTS (BLACK) AND ACCORDING TO THE TEACHER'S JUDGMENT (WHITE). THUS, THE PUPIL RANKED 29 ON TEST RESULTS WAS RANKED 8 BY THE TEACHER.

PROGRAM OF SUPERVISION 17

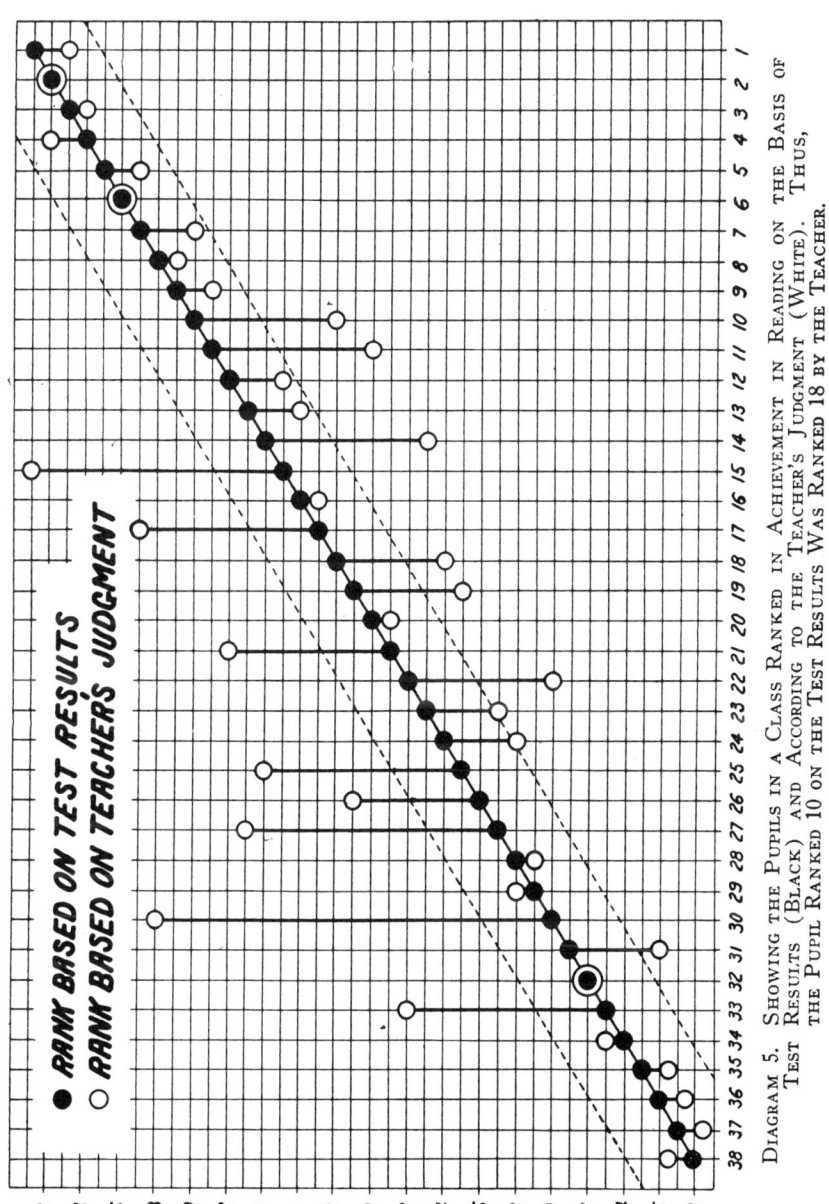

DIAGRAM 5. SHOWING THE PUPILS IN A CLASS RANKED IN ACHIEVEMENT IN READING ON THE BASIS OF TEST RESULTS (BLACK) AND ACCORDING TO THE TEACHER'S JUDGMENT (WHITE). THUS, THE PUPIL RANKED 10 ON THE TEST RESULTS WAS RANKED 18 BY THE TEACHER.

cases it might prove after consideration by the group of teachers that their judgment had been handicapping the pupil. An older dull child may have been pushed beyond his capacity to achieve merely because of his age, while a young mentally gifted pupil may have been held back because his capacity had never been discovered.

These diagrams were particularly helpful in selecting individual children for study and in indicating to a teacher her general tendency to over-rate or to under-rate her pupils.

SUGGESTED IMPROVEMENTS IN PROCEDURE

Suggested future improvements in general procedure follow:

1. Initial care should be taken to secure the interest and coöperation of the teaching staff as well as that of the superintendent, principals and supervisors. Several early meetings with the latter group mentioned, before the measurement program was undertaken, had given assurance that the desire for its addition to the system was sincere and that coöperation from them could be depended upon. Probably the greatest mistake made during the program lay in assuming that the teachers in the system already possessed the same desire and will to coöperate, or that this would be secured by the superintendent and principals of schools. What actually happened was that a few teachers were openly and defiantly antagonistic to the entire program throughout. Most were willing to follow the various steps decided upon, but did so without particular enthusiasm. None worked as actively for the program as the few worked against it.

Initial securing of desire to coöperate on the part of a large majority of the staff probably strikes one of the most important psychological factors affecting the degree of success of a measurement program. Initial questions should have been secured from the teaching staff if possible as well as from the administrative staff. Interest and the will to coöperate should not have been assumed. Sustained interest throughout the year and successive years, in any measurement program, is, in all probability, as dependent for success upon initial motive as is endeavor in any other field. A report, no matter how rich in content and suggestion, which answers questions that have never been asked by the teacher or staff concerned runs big chances of being carefully laid away in a desk drawer to be read or studied "when there is time."

With the best intentions in the world "time" seldom is found and the possible aid is easily forgotten because it was given unbidden.

It may be of interest to the reader to have reported an instance of this sort that took place during the present program. A plan for some remedial work in a certain study needing attention—as shown by results found—had been mimeographed and a copy sent to each member of the staff. Some time later, during a series of group meetings, the teachers were asked to what extent the suggestions had proved helpful. Only blank expressions met the question and without exception all claimed that they had received no such report. The second group gave a similar response. It was known that the reports had been distributed as had been requested, so the third group was asked to search their desks. In a very few minutes all but one returned with the copies.

2. Clerical assistance should be furnished for the director of a measurement program. Teachers resent giving the time required for scoring and tabulation of results, and, if these are left entirely to the director, little time remains for attention to the supervisory measures that should accompany every series of measurements.

It is also important that a report of the results of any measurement program should follow its administration as soon as possible. This is desirable from two standpoints, namely, keeping interest alive and allowing for a maximum amount of follow-up work. It is probably safe to say that any amount of time spent by the supervisor of a measurement program on the clerical work connected with it operates as educational loss to the system engaging him.

CHAPTER III

EVALUATION OF THE SUPERVISION

Any measurement program ought to justify itself, in part, by showing educational gains on the part of the staff in terms of such matters as:
1. Keener interest in current educational problems.
2. Better understanding of the tools of their profession, such as methods, curricula, available diagnostic and remedial measures, etc.
3. Greater focusing of attention on balance of emphasis in the various phases of instruction.
4. A more scientific attitude on the part of the staff toward their profession, as shown by a desire and willingness to coöperate pleasantly in research and experiment being carried on for the purpose of improvement in education in general.

Since there is no objective means of determining the full amount of gain or loss from this professional standpoint, an estimation is all that is possible at present. Careful consideration of the professional aspects of the program mentioned resulted in the decision that considerable gain was shown by all principals and supervisors of schools and by a few teachers. Some of the evidences were as follows:
1. Immediately after the completion of this program, steps were taken by the superintendent to secure a person who could supervise the continuation of measurement in the schools.
2. Special provision was made for the instruction of the special problem children who had been previously chosen on the basis of the testing results.
3. The junior high school principal had found the results of the intelligence tests such an aid to him in his classification problems that he undertook alone the subsequent measurement of all sixth grade children in the school system, so as to have records available upon the pupils' arrival in his school in the fall.
4. The principal of the high school asked that intelligence tests

be given in his school. These were judged to be so helpful that later both principal and teachers asked assistance in a program of prognostic testing.

5. The principals of the elementary and junior high schools voluntarily requested training in the administration and interpretation of both group and individual tests, and gave sufficient time to such training to be approved.

6. The superintendent of schools initiated a plan for the entire teaching staff to receive an elementary course in measurement. He made himself personally responsible for assembling the teachers to receive such instruction in a series of ten meetings.

A measurement program will also need to justify itself in showing greater educational progress on the part of the pupils. The following procedure represents a crude method of measuring these greater educational gains due to the program of measurement:

1. First, all important factors in the educational progress of the community were considered to see if changes other than the addition of the measurement program had been made in the system's educational scheme which might operate to create gain or loss. In this situation, the superintendent, principals of schools, special supervisors, teachers, general equipment, number of pupils measured, etc., remained essentially the same as in the years just previous. The measurement program appeared to be the only significant new element in the situation. Therefore it seemed fair to assume that any differential gain or loss could be ascribed wholly or largely to the measurement program.

The term "differential gain" is used because the process to be described does not measure the actual gain made during the year by identical pupils. The eighth grade pupils graduated and were not measured the second time. The second grade was promoted into the third grade, where it was measured in 1923, although it had not previously been measured. The term as used henceforth will mean superiority of the second group over the first presumably equal and comparable group.

2. The second step was to determine the total gain or loss in subject age units between the two periods of measurement, October, 1922, and October, 1923.

Table I (p. 23) gives the results found in this respect. Thus, the total reading units found in October, 1922, was 134,958. This total was found simply by adding the reading ages for all the pupils in all the classes in grades three to eight inclusive. The same process was repeated for the results of measurement in October, 1923. The total reading units found this time was 159,053. The simple arithmetic difference between the two totals was 24,095 units. This amount represented the gain in reading units during the year. The gain in units for each subject shown in the table was determined in the same manner.

3. The third step was to correct the total subject unit gains owing to the fact that there were thirty more pupils tested in October, 1923, than in October, 1922. The 134,958 reading age units, for example, were made by 986 pupils, whereas the 159,053 reading age units were made by 1016 pupils, and similarly for the total subject units in arithmetic, spelling, composition and penmanship.

The final corrected gain in reading, shown in the last column of Table I, was computed as follows:

$$159,053 \div 1016 = 156.5$$
$$156.5 \times 30 = 4\,695$$
$$24,095 - 4695 = 19,400$$

The final corrected gain in arithmetic was computed in like manner as follows:

$$153,971 \div 1016 = 151.5$$
$$151.5 \times 30 = 4\,545$$
$$9\,068 - 4545 = 4\,523$$

The final corrected gains in the other subjects were computed according to the same method. The assumption of this method is that the 30 pupils are a random sampling of the 1016 pupils. As a matter of fact, 28 of them were in grades 3, 4, 5, and 6, and only 2 of them in grades 7 and 8. Since there were 685 pupils in the lower grades and 331 in the two upper grades, the lower grades had an undue proportion of the 30 pupils. This means that the corrections made are probably too large, thus causing the corrected gains shown in Table I to be conservative.

4. The fourth step was to calculate the significance of the corrected subject unit gains. One way to do this might be to calculate the financial value of these gains, using the cost of producing one unit of gain as the unit of measurement. Another method

EVALUATION OF THE SUPERVISION

would be to calculate how much this gain would mean if concentrated in one pupil. Both have been done. The latter is reported below.

If a typical pupil were to continue in a typical school and were to make the typical growth of 12 reading age units each year, it would require 1617 years for him to acquire the 19,400 excess reading units which can reasonably be ascribed to the measurement program. Stated differently, it might be said that the special growth in reading ability produced by the measurement program is equal to a typical year's growth of 1617 typical pupils attending during that year a typical school.

The significance of the corrected gains in other subjects could be expressed in a similar manner.

TABLE I

TOTAL SUBJECT UNITS AND TOTAL SUBJECT UNIT GAINS FOUND AS A RESULT
OF THE TWO MEASUREMENT PROGRAMS
OCTOBER 1922 AND OCTOBER 1923

Subject	Total Subject Units Oct. 1922 Grades 3 to 8	Total Subject Units Oct. 1923 Grades 3 to 8	Total Subject Unit Gains Oct. 1923 Grades 3 to 8	Corrected Subject Unit Gains Grades 3 to 8
Reading	134,958	159,053	24,095	19,400
Arithmetic	144,903	153,971	9,068	4,523
Spelling	143,950	153,200	9,250	4,726
Composition	142,259	156,146	13,889	9,278
Penmanship	119,521	130,856	11,335	7,471

The more important criticisms of the technique follow:

1. Was the factor of normal growth that naturally takes place in all school systems every year taken into account?

Those who ask this question believe that what they call normal growth was responsible for some of the total gain in units.

Imagine for a moment that school systems could be measured in inches. By "normal growth" these critics mean that a system measuring ten inches this year will just normally measure more inches next year and the next, and so on indefinitely. It would be gratifying to believe that the schools in every city grow better and better each year, but as yet we have no objective proof that this invariably happens.

On the other hand, we have some evidence that the annual growth in the efficiency of school systems in their teaching of the fundamentals is very, very small. [3]

Furthermore, the very largeness of the amount of the gain negatives the suggestion that normal growth in efficiency through the years is responsible for it. A small amount of gain might be ascribed to such a cause, but not an amount such as is revealed in Table I. Consider reading, for example. If normal growth is responsible, normal growth in teaching efficiency causes, say, a typical eight-year-old pupil in 1923 to read better than a typical eight-year-old in 1922 by 19 months of reading age. Common observation shows that no such striking differences are revealed by two successive typical eight-year-old groups, or any other age groups for that matter. When the typical eight-year-old continues in school until he graduates from the elementary school at, say, fourteen years of age, he will ordinarily have a reading age of 12 times 14, *i.e.*, 168 months. On an assumption of a normal acceleration of 19 reading months each year, our typical eight-year-old will have a reading age of 282 months at the time he graduates. No sane person would claim that fourteen-year-old graduates today read 114 months better than fourteen-year-old graduates six years ago. Clearly some cause other than normal annual growth in teaching efficiency is responsible for so striking an improvement in the reading ability of the pupils.

2. At the time of the second measurement program in October, 1923, the original eighth grade had dropped out and the original second grade had been added to the unit, grades 3 to 8 inclusive, that was measured in October, 1922. Does this invalidate results?

Measuring the same children was not necessary in this problem. Since the general characteristics of the community had remained the same, it is safe to assume that the general characteristics of the new unit measured, grades 3 to 8 inclusive, were comparable with the original unit, especially after allowances for differences in number of children in the two units had been made.

3. Might not relative loss of units in some subjects mean actual gain on the whole and should they not be credited as gain?

Diagram 6 furnishes an example of this nature, where it is shown that, as the result of recommendations made, the year's work

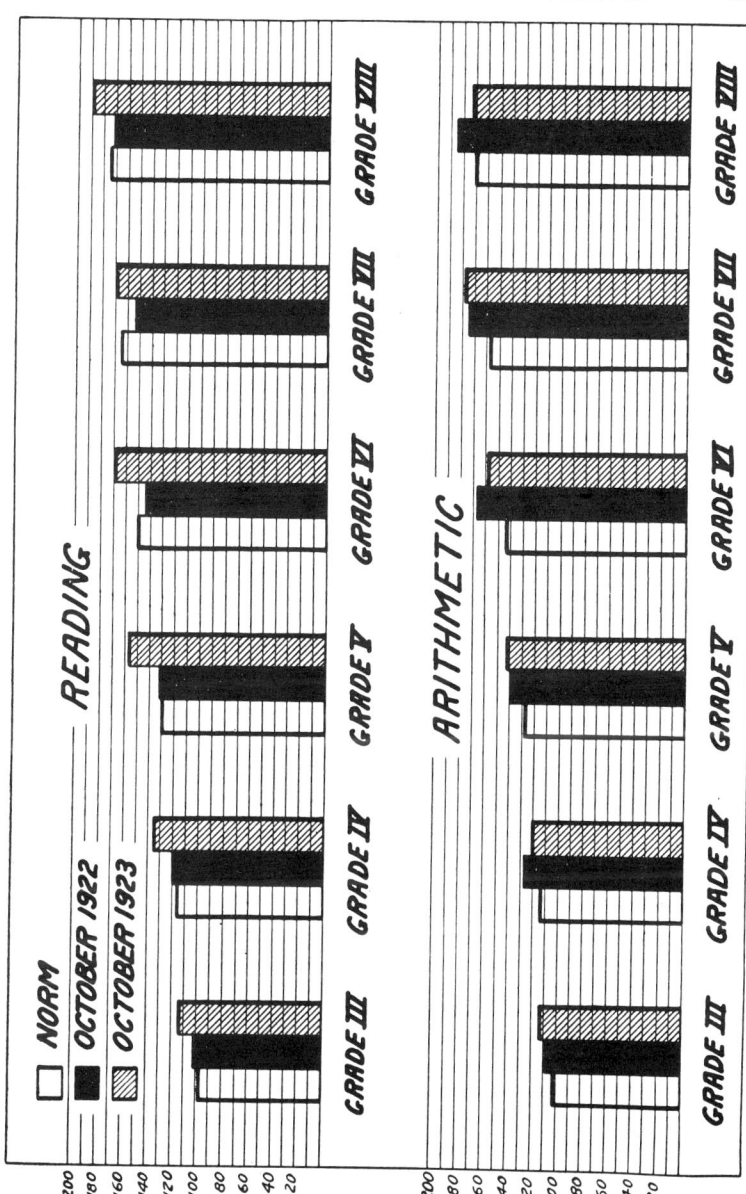

Diagram 6. Comparison of the Achievement in Reading and Arithmetic by the Various Grades, for October 1922 and October 1923, With the Standard Norm.

showed better balance between achievement in the fundamentals in arithmetic and achievement in reading for comprehension. The first measurement program revealed the fact that the average achievement in arithmetic far excelled the norm in all grades in the system and that the relative achievement in reading was below that which should be expected. A study of the factors involved showed that relatively too much time and emphasis were being given to arithmetic and too little to reading. Recognition by the staff of the need for better balance brought about the desired results, and ideally this change should in itself be credited as educational gain.

Finally, it seems highly probable that the measurement program should be credited with a large and significant gain in the achievement of pupils. Furthermore, the effect of some very important changes due to the presence in the system of the measurement program could not be measured. Some of these were a more intelligent interest on the part of the principals and teachers in what constituted desirable outcomes in education, better methods of instruction, etc., and on the part of the pupils the building of more efficient methods of study, etc. Should not some gain be added for these changes?

The amount of gain in these educational changes was to some extent measured by the tests in their effect on the gain of power on the part of the pupils in the use of the skills, but it is very probable that not all of these gains were registered by the tests. Furthermore, their permanence causes one to wonder if the amount of measured gain brought about as a result of the above supervisory measures should not be multiplied by a certain number of years.

PART TWO

MEASURING TEACHING

CHAPTER IV

STAGES IN THE EVOLUTION OF METHODS

FIRST STAGE—GENERAL IMPRESSION METHOD

In the evolution of methods for the measuring of teaching efficiency there have been three well defined stages. The first of these is what has been called the general impression method. According to this plan the supervisory officer observed the teacher for varying periods of time and then recorded for him a single total score.

The chief defects of this method, which still persists quite universally, are probably the following:

1. The method is deficient in validity. Validity requires that the method should measure exactly what it purports to measure. With no controlling specifications to guide the judges, we have no way of knowing just what they think they are measuring when expressing judgments. Ability to "get along" socially in the community may be the basis for one supervisor's ratings. Pleasing personality may guide another, while desirable changes in the pupils and little regard for the personal make-up of a teacher may determine another judge's decision.

2. The method is deficient in objectivity. To be objective there must be close agreement between different judges. With no common bases for judgment, different supervisors may vary widely in judgments of the same teacher, or a given supervisor may judge different teachers on different bases. Minor details may influence a decision either favorably or unfavorably. A supervisor may feel extremely lenient when applying his standards of judgment on one day. At another time, while applying the same standards, he may react in the opposite direction. The general impression method does not at any point prevent him from changing at will his stand-

ards or his methods and thus altering results. It may even be true that he has not formulated in his mind either standards or methods for his own procedure.

SECOND STAGE—SCORE CARD METHOD

Elliott's [4] *Score Card for Measuring the Merits of Teachers* is an early example of the second stage of teacher measurement. Its first division seeks to measure individual efficiency, with headings such as Physical Efficiency, Moral-Native Efficiency, Administrative Efficiency, Social Efficiency, etc. Its second division has one heading, Supervisory Efficiency. Under these headings are listed forty-two traits considered essential to successful teaching.

A certain number of points were to be given for perfection in each of the traits. The supervisor was then to deduct from this maximum stated amounts in accordance with his judgment of each teacher's deficiency in the particular trait. Out of a possible ten points to be given for any trait, 2 were to be deducted for very slight deficiency, 4 for slight, 6 for marked, 7 for very marked and 8 for extreme.

Another example of the second stage is the *Score Card of the New York Bureau of Municipal Research* [5]. It sought a qualitative description of the teacher rather than a numerical rating.

This card was divided into two sections. The first sought an index of the teacher's personality by requesting that a check mark be placed opposite certain descriptive terms so as to note their presence or lack of presence. Some of these terms were vigorous, weak, poised, nervous, neat, etc. The second division aimed to secure an index of the teaching ability of each individual. For example, one of its sections asked for the degree to which a teacher's questions were (1) thought-provoking, (2) calling for facts, (3) suggesting the answer, (4) answered by "yes" or "no," (5) irrelevant, (6) not definite—vague. The degree of presence of each quality was shown by a check placed in one of four columns headed respectively, not at all, slight, medium, and notable.

Rugg's [6] *Rating Scale for Judging Teachers in Service* is an example of a score card primarily designed to secure self-improvement through numerical self-rating.

Qualities; IV. Qualities of Growth and Keeping Up-to-date; V.

This score card has five main headings: I. Skill in Teaching; II. Skill in the Mechanics of Managing a Class; III. Team Work

Personal and Social Qualities. One of the questions under I. Skill in Teaching is, To what extent has he insight into "how children learn"? Under this are three sub-questions: (1) Does he keep the discussion within the pupils' comprehension? (2) Does he endeavor to discover pupils' difficulties by keeping records of errors and studying these? (3) Does he adapt discussion to individual differences in pupils? All questions were to be answered by checking in the columns provided at the right, "low," "average," or "high."

The second section of this card is for the use of principals and superintendents in giving to the teacher a rating by direct comparison. On the back of the card, careful instructions are given, first, for the construction of a rating scale in any system, and second, as to how to rate teachers on the scale.

This section of Rugg's Rating Scale embodies what is often referred to as the Human-Ladder Scale, the Man-to-Man Comparison Scale or the Direct Comparison Scale. A brief description of the steps necessary in the construction of a rating scale as given by Rugg on his score card follows:

1. Write down a list of 25 or 30 teachers ranging from the very best to the very poorest in your acquaintance, for each of whom you can give judgments.

2. Arrange this list in rank order of merit from the "best" to the "poorest," separately for each of the five groups of qualities to be judged.

3. Select the five persons to occupy five positions on the scale in each group of qualities. These positions should be designated in the order of "best," "poorest," "average," "poorer than average," and "better than average."

4. Assign numerical values of 38, 30, 22, 14 and 6 to each of these five, respectively. These values were chosen so as to allow considerable opportunity to assign values between the set points. The rating was then to be made for one group of qualities at a time, giving each person a stated number of points for that quality. This was done by comparing the person's qualities directly with those of others whose names appear on the scale.

These and similar score cards have not met with general approval. All still remain too subjective to permit any great degree of confidence in the results obtained.

THIRD STAGE—OBJECTIVE MEASUREMENT METHOD

The objective measurement stage itself falls readily into two periods:

1. The first is the period when a class was measured, usually near the end of the year, and the results reported in relation to the norms as given in the manual accompanying the test in question. The pupils were "meeting the norm," or "not meeting it," and their teacher was judged accordingly.

Several fundamental defects accompanied this method of measuring the teacher. One defect was that over-ageness or under-ageness of the pupils in any given class was not taken into account. Other things being equal, the teacher of a chronologically older class has greater advantage than the teacher of a younger class. Before the efficiency of these two teachers can be justly compared allowance must be made for this factor.

Another defect was that no provision was made for an initial test. Hence, there was no means of segregating gain made this year by one teacher from that made by another teacher during the previous year.

Again, no account was taken of the mental ages of pupils—that is, their capacity to achieve; or the brightness of the children—that is, an index of their rate of growth. Other things being equal, it is not fair to rate a teacher of a class with high mental age in comparison with a teacher of a class with lower mental age, when the rating is being done on the basis of the achievement of the class. Also, it is not fair to compare a teacher of a bright class with a teacher of a dull class, when the rating is on the basis of the amount of growth produced per unit of time.

2. The second period in the development of the objective measurement method gave us the Accomplishment Ratio (AR) formula by Franzen [7] and the Achievement Quotient (AQ) formula by Monroe and Buckingham [8]. Similar results are yielded by the two formulæ, which are:

$$\text{AQ or AR} = \frac{\text{Subject Age}}{\text{Mental Age}} \times 100.$$

By removing emphasis from absolute accomplishment as shown by the test to relative accomplishment based upon the pupil's capacity to achieve, the teacher was more properly rated. The AR formula eliminates the disturbing factors of over- or under-ageness and mental age in the measurement of teachers. But it does not eliminate error due to the absence of initial test.

To overcome this difficulty Franzen proposed the AR Teaching Efficiency formula which forms the basis for this study. Pupils were measured at the beginning and at the close of a definite period of time, and the gain or loss in their AR's during this particular period was credited to the teacher in charge. The general form of the formula follows:

$$\text{Teacher Efficiency} = \text{Final AR} - \text{Initial AR}$$

The chief virtue of this method lies in the fact that it focuses attention in education more definitely upon desirable changes made in children. Its main weakness lies in the fact that as yet we cannot measure directly and can only partially measure indirectly many of the outcomes in education, some of the unmeasured outcomes being probably among the most important of all.

CHAPTER V

COMPUTATION OF EFFICIENCY MEASURES FOR EACH TEACHER

SOURCE AND NATURE OF THE DATA FOR THE COMPUTATIONS

The remainder of Part II deals with the measuring of teaching efficiency. The detailed problems connected with this major problem are stated in Chapter I. The data upon which this study is based are taken from an urban and also from a rural situation. The urban data are those collected as described in Part I. The corresponding rural data were collected in the schools of Queen Anne's County, Maryland.

In these rural schools, exactly the same tests were administered as were used in the urban situation. They were administered by the superintendent, supervising teacher, and attendance officer. All three had given a series of tests in the same county for three years, and were trained in the standard procedure that was used.

The tests were scored by two principals of elementary schools and the clerk of the supervision department. These scores were checked by the supervising teacher, the attendance officer, a clerk, two principals of elementary schools and the clerk of the supervision department. No paper was checked by the same person who had scored it originally.

One difference in the two situations from the standpoint of tests was that the interval between the two testing programs was six months in the rural, from the first Monday in October, 1922, to the second Monday in April, 1923, whereas it was twelve months, from October, 1922, to October, 1923, in the case of urban testing. A second difference lay in the fact that the rural situation had had three previous organized testing programs, whereas the urban had given little attention to testing.

The remainder of this section will be devoted to a statement of the general rural conditions. The organization of the schools in

EFFICIENCY MEASURES FOR EACH TEACHER

these two systems differed as do most urban and rural systems. In the urban, a different teacher was provided for each grade. The rural presents the usual rural plan. There were one-, two- and three-or-more-room schools. For convenience, the last will be spoken of hereafter as three-room schools.

The one-room schools varied in enrollment from small to medium sized classes with one teacher in charge of all. However, even the smallest of these schools provided for all grades from one to eight inclusive.

The two-room schools provided for the same range of grades, but with two teachers in charge. One was responsible for grades one to four inclusive and one for grades five to eight inclusive.

The third group, which was made up of the three-room and more than three-room schools, followed the same general plan. One teacher had charge of grades one to three inclusive, a second of grades four and five, and another of six and seven or six, seven and eight. Only one school in the group provided more than three teachers for the eight grades. In this school there was a different teacher for each of the grades furnishing data for this study.

COMPUTATION OF TEACHER EFFICIENCY MEASURES IN EACH SUBJECT

The process for the computation of an efficiency measure for each teacher in each subject is illustrated in Table II. This table shows the nature of the data available or made available for the teacher of this particular one-room school. A similar table was constructed for each teacher of a one-room school, and for each class in the two-room, three-room and urban schools. How the data shown in each column of Table II were secured is told below in order of column:

1. Because children in several grades were located in the same room in the one-, two- and three-room schools of the rural situation, it was desirable to record the grade for each pupil. It is to be found in the first column.

2. In the second column of this series the initial chronological age in months is given. This is the pupil's age at the time of the first series of measurements. In computing this figure, fifteen days or over were called one month, while anything under fifteen days was discarded.

3. The initial mental age in months is recorded in the third column. The score made by each pupil on the National Intelli-

TABLE II—COMPUTATION OF EFFICIENCY
School 7-5. Three-room

Grade	Initial Chron. Age	Initial Mental Age	Intell. Quotient	Final Mental Age	Initial Read. AR	Final Read. AR	Read. AR Gain	Initial Arith. AR	Final Arith. AR
1	2	3	4	5	6	7	8	9	10
6	136	149	110	156	95	87	− 8	109	116
6	165	139	85	144	97	106	9	117	130
6	157	112	72	116	96	122	26	121	145
6	143	172	121	179	79	107	28	83	94
6	162	132	82	137	103	99	− 4	103	110
7	162	171	106	177	86	99	13	91	88
7	172	147	86	152	92	100	8	106	111
7	191	165	87	170	89	93	4	106	102
7	131	168	129	176	91	96	5	116	103
8	159	204	129	212	86	85	− 1	89	104
8	182	209	115	216	84	94	10	93	90
8	156	166	107	172	102	112	10	109	101
8	171	182	107	188	93	75	−18	81	86

Averages................103.................. 6.3.............4.3
Composite Efficiency = 18.27

gence Test was transmuted into a mental age by means of a table furnished with the testing manual.

4. Column four of this series gives us the intelligence quotient for each pupil. It was computed by dividing the mental age for each pupil found in the third column by the chronological age found in the second column and multiplying by one hundred. This computation for the first pupil follows:

$$(149 \div 136)100 = 110$$

EFFICIENCY MEASURES FOR EACH TEACHER

MEASURES FOR A TEACHER
Rural. Grades 6, 7, 8

Arith. AR Gain	Initial Spell. AR	Final Spell. AR	Spell. AR Gain	Initial Comp. AR	Final Comp. AR	Comp. AR Gain	Initial Pen. AR	Final Pen. AR	Pen. AR Gain
11	*12*	*13*	*14*	*15*	*16*	*17*	*18*	*19*	*20*
7	95	95	0	112	89	−23	73	112	39
13	99	97	− 2	84	97	13	67	99	32
24	108	113	5	105	101	− 4	83	81	− 2
11	77	78	1	81	78	− 3	63	79	16
7	106	102	− 4	106	102	− 4	71	104	33
− 3	77	77	0	81	79	− 2	64	62	− 2
5	99	100	1	95	110	15	74	115	41
− 4	86	87	1	101	119	18	86	118	32
−13	84	84	0	83	115	32	55	62	7
15	79	76	− 3	82	114	32	86	95	9
− 3	72	71	− 1	80	112	32	112	81	−31
− 8	92	89	− 3	84	140	56	86	102	16
5	82	82	0	92	128	36	78	107	29

................−0.4.............15.2......................16.8

5. The final mental age of each pupil at the time of the second measurement program is the last of this series of measures recorded. Because the intelligence quotient for each individual is approximately constant, it was unnecessary to administer another intelligence measure to secure a second mental age. The following formula was used to compute the final mental age:

Final mental age = initial mental age ÷ the number of months elapsing between the two periods of measurement × the pupil's intelligence quotient ÷ by 100.

Using the first pupil's records again we have the following:

$$149 + \frac{6 \times 110}{100} = 156.$$

The number of months elapsing in the urban situation was 12 instead of 6. This completes the intelligence measures used in the study of teaching efficiency.

6. Initial reading accomplishment ratio is the pupil's initial status in reading at the time of the first measurement program. The first step in the computation of this measure was to transmute the score made by each pupil on the initial Thorndike-McCall Reading Scale into a reading age by means of the table given in the manual for these tests. This initial reading age was then divided by the initial mental age of the pupil in order to secure the Initial Reading Accomplishment Ratio, the measure recorded in the sixth column. Subject ages were recorded on another group of class tabulations, so that, with the exception of the mental age, no figures appear for any age on these tabulations. The formula for this step reads:

Initial RAR = (Initial Reading Age ÷ Initial Mental Age) × 100.

For the first pupil whose records appear on the tabulation sheet, 95 is the record thus computed.

7. The seventh column contains the final Reading Accomplishment Ratio. This was determined by the following formula:

Final RAR = (Final RA ÷ Final MA) × 100.

The unknown element in this formula, namely, final reading age, was found by testing the pupils with the Thorndike-McCall Reading Scale at the close of the six months, and by converting their score on this test into a Reading Age in accordance with a table in the manual accompanying this test. Thus the final mental age was computed from the initial mental age and Intelligence Quotient, but the final reading age was determined anew by means of a test.

8. The eighth column shows the change, either gain or loss, in each pupil's Reading Accomplishment Ratio that occurred during the six months. Thus, the first pupil started the year with a Reading Accomplishment Ratio of 95. Six months later his Read-

EFFICIENCY MEASURES FOR EACH TEACHER 37

ing Accomplishment Ratio was 87. This represents a loss of 8 points as shown in the table.

This does not mean that the pupil's ability actually went backward, though it is possible for actual retrogression to occur. Any half-hour reading test is so unreliable that errors of measurement might show a particular pupil to have retrogressed, when he may actually have gone forward or stood still. However, the more important coefficients of correlation to be reported later are based upon mean AR gains and not upon individual AR gains. The effect of chance errors of measurement tend to be eliminated in the calculation of means. It should be pointed out that any pupil who makes the normal progress expected of him in the light of his intelligence will not show a gain in Reading Accomplishment Ratio. Instead, his gain will be zero.

This is why the Accomplishment Ratio unit has been used in this study to measure the efficiency of a teacher. This unit, in effect, is a sort of handicap unit. The teacher of a bright class is given a heavy handicap by this unit, whereas the teacher of a dull class is given an advantage exactly commensurate with the intellectual inferiority of the pupils. This operates to give every teacher a standard class of children irrespective of their actual capacity to learn.

9. The ninth column gives the initial Arithmetic Accomplishment Ratio, computed as follows:

Initial AAR = (Initial Arithmetic Age ÷ Initial Mental Age) × 100

The determination of initial mental age has already been explained. The initial arithmetic age was secured by giving the Woody-McCall Arithmetic Test and converting the crude score made by each child into an arithmetic age by means of a table.

10. The tenth column contains the final Arithmetic Accomplishment Ratio, computed as follows:

Final AAR = (Final Arithmetic Age ÷ Final Mental Age) × 100

The computation of final mental age has already been explained. The final arithmetic age was secured by actually giving a second arithmetic test at the end of the six months and converting the score obtained into an arithmetic age.

11. The eleventh column gives the change that occurred in six months' time in the Arithmetic Accomplishment Ratio. In the case

of the first pupil the change was zero, which, interpreted, means that this pupil made just the progress expected of him in view of his intelligence.

In like manner, steps 12, 13, 14, 15, 16, 17, 18, 19, and 20—initial Spelling Accomplishment Ratio, final Spelling Accomplishment Ratio, Spelling Accomplishment Ratio Change, initial Composition Accomplishment Ratio, final Composition Accomplishment Ratio, Composition Accomplishment Ratio Change, initial Penmanship Accomplishment Ratio, final Penmanship Accomplishment Ratio, and Penmanship Accomplishment Ratio Change—were computed and tabulated in columns 11, 12, 13, 14, 15, 16, 17, 18, 19 and 20, respectively.

21. The twenty-first step was the computation of the mean, with regard to signs, of the Accomplishment Ratio changes for each subject. The mean change in reading was 6.3, in arithmetic 4.3, in spelling — 0.4, in composition 15.2, and in penmanship 16.8. These are, in order, measures of the teacher's efficiency in teaching reading, arithmetic, spelling, composition and penmanship.

The procedure described above entailed the scoring of 21,600 test papers and the tabulation of the results. It entailed the calculation and tabulation of 1,800 chronological ages, 3,600 mental ages, 1,800 Intelligence Quotients, 18,000 subject ages, 18,000 Subject Accomplishment Ratios, and 9,000 Subject Accomplishment Ratio differences. The foregoing does not include the additional calculations involved in the determination of means, variabilities, correlations and the like yet to be reported. Even so, the procedure required a minimum of 73,800 separate calculations.

COMPUTATION OF COMPOSITE MEASURE OF TEACHER'S EFFICIENCY

The last step was the combination of these separate efficiency measures for the teacher in the various subjects into a composite measure of his efficiency in teaching all of these subjects, weighting each subject in accordance with the worth of producing each additional unit of AR change in that subject.

In computing this composite mean AR it would not be proper simply to add the mean AR's for the various subjects. To do this would be, in effect, to say that an AR unit in penmanship is worth an AR unit in reading. But the consensus of opinion of competent judges regarded reading units as worth more than penmanship units, as shown in table below. In constructing the composite mean AR, each mean AR was weighted in accordance with the estimates made by these judges as to the relative worth of the various subjects.

Weights, when composites are being computed, are decided on different bases in different situations. But weighting is always effected through alterations in variability. Hence, frequency distributions were constructed for all the mean AR changes in reading for all the rural classes. Similar distributions were made for like measures for urban data separately. Then, the SD or variability of this rural distribution was computed, and similarly for the urban distribution. In like manner SD's were computed for mean AR changes in arithmetic, spelling, composition and penmanship for rural and then for urban data. The following tabular arrangement illustrates how the SD's were used in conjunction with the worth judgments of the judges to determine the multipliers that would have to be used to give to each subject the weight to which it was entitled in computing the composite.

	Reading	Arithmetic	Spelling	Composition	Penmanship
Worth estimate.......	23	16	11	11	10
SD (rural)...........	8.3	4.2	2.9	7.7	7.4
Multiplier (rural).....	.7	1	1	.3	.3
Weight given (rural)...	5.8	4.2	2.9	2.3	2.2
SD (urban)..........	4.0	4.1	2.9	9.7	10.9
Multiplier (urban)....	1.5	1	1	.3	.2
Weight given (urban)..	6.0	4.1	2.9	2.9	2.2

It will be noticed in the foregoing that the worth estimate is 23 for reading, 16 for arithmetic, etc. The actual weights given were not 23, 16, etc., but 5.8, 4.2., etc., for the rural data. The numbers 5.8, 4.2, etc., are not identical with 23, 16, etc., but the weights actually given bear approximately the same ratio to each other as the weights desired bear to each other. Such differences as exist are due to the fact that convenient one-decimal multipliers were used. In like manner, multipliers were chosen for the urban data that brought the weights given into the same approximate ratio with each other as the weights desired, namely, 23, 16, etc., bear to each other, respectively.

The data of Table II may be used to illustrate how these multipliers were used in computing a composite measure of a teacher's efficiency. The final formula used was:

$$\text{Composite Efficiency} = (.7 \times 6.3) + (1 \times 4.3) + (1 \times -.4) \\ + (.3 \times 15.2) + (.3 \times 16.8) \\ = 18.27$$

The first of the two numbers in each parenthesis is the multiplier, and the second is the mean AR gain for the class in reading, arithmetic, etc., respectively. The composite efficiency, so computed, namely 18.27, is recorded at the bottom of Table II.

In like manner, composite efficiency measures were computed for all the rural teachers and all the urban teachers. When the composite efficiency scores were being computed for the urban teachers, the urban multipliers were used instead of the rural multipliers. Otherwise the process was identical.

CHAPTER VI

CORRELATION BETWEEN OBJECTIVE EFFICIENCY MEASURES

TO WHAT EXTENT IS A TEACHER'S EFFICIENCY IN TEACHING READING AN INDEX OF HIS EFFICIENCY IN TEACHING OTHER SUBJECTS?

The preceding chapter describes a method whereby a series of efficiency measures was computed for a number of rural and urban teachers. To answer the above question some method needed to be employed to determine the proportionality between the two series of efficiency measures for the same teachers for reading and, say, arithmetic, and then for reading and spelling, and so on for all the subjects for which there are available efficiency measures.

Should both rural and urban teachers be considered as one group in determining this desired proportionality? To do so would lay one open to the criticism of having used heterogeneous data, thus spuriously increasing the true amount of proportionality. It cannot be denied that the urban teachers measured over a twelve-month period were not strictly comparable to rural teachers measured over six months. Furthermore, it is possible that differences in the nature and amount of the proportionality for the two groups may be fully as significant as the nature and amount of proportionality for either group or both combined. Hence, it was decided to treat the two sets of data separately.

Should all the rural teachers be treated as a homogeneous group or should one-room teachers be treated as one group, two-room teachers as another group, three-or-more-room teachers as still another group? The three groups are homogeneous with respect to administration, supervision and ruralness. As data to be presented later will show, there are certain significant respects in which they are not homogeneous. Nevertheless the differences did not appear to be large enough to justify the great increase in time required to treat the three groups separately. Furthermore, and most important in this situation, mixing the groups is defensible even if it increase the amount of proportionality, because the heterogeneity is coextensive with the area or range of practical decisions about teachers. Even so, scatter diagrams were prepared before any computations were begun, in order to discover whether mixing the groups would materially alter the amount of proportionality or conceal significant differences among the three groups. In no instance did the scatter diagrams reveal differences large enough to justify separate computations.

As already mentioned, the first step in the process of determining the proportionality between any two of the series of measures for the rural or urban teachers was to plot a scatter diagram. In doing this, the mean RAR gains were assigned to one axis and the mean AAR gains to the other. In plotting the pair for each teacher, a dot was used to indicate a one-room teacher, a cross to indicate a two-room teacher, and a circle to indicate a three-room teacher. In this way a brief inspection told whether the general trend of the diagram was different for the different types of teachers. In like manner diagrams were plotted with mean RAR gains and mean SAR gains as the two variables, and so on for composition and penmanship. The statistical measure employed for determining the amount of proportionality between each two series of data was the product-moment coefficient of correlation. The process is described in any standard book on statistical methods. The meaning of the coefficients of correlation yielded by this process will be taken up below.

The coefficients of correlation between reading and the other subjects together with the mean of all the coefficients follow:

	Arithmetic	Spelling	Composition	Penmanship	Mean
Reading (rural).......	.12	.23	.28	−.11	.13
Reading (urban)......	.43	.24	.22	.15	.26

There are three approaches for the interpretation of the above coefficients of correlation, usually designated r. The first approach is through the size of the r's themselves. An r may be any size from -1.0 through 0 to $+1.0$. When the degree of each teacher's efficiency in teaching reading coincides exactly with the degree of that teacher's efficiency in teaching arithmetic, the r is $+1.0$. The correlation in this case is said to be positive and perfect. When the r is -1.0, the relationship is also perfect, but it is inverse, *i.e.*, to be efficient as a teacher of reading is to be just to that degree inefficient as a teacher of arithmetic, and vice versa. When there is no relationship either positive or negative between the two series of efficiency measures, the r is 0. An r may be any fraction from -1.0 to 0, according to the degree of inverseness that exists, or any fraction from 0 to $+1.0$.

From the foregoing point of view the actually obtained r's shown above may be interpreted as follows:

1. There is a very slight positive correlation between efficiency in teaching reading and efficiency in teaching respectively arithmetic, spelling and composition. This conclusion is true for both rural and urban teachers.

2. For the rural teachers there is very slight negative correlation between efficiency in teaching reading and efficiency in teaching penmanship. This means that the more successful teachers of reading in these rural schools tended to be the less successful teachers of penmanship.

The existence of this negative r provokes speculation as to its cause. Is it due to the fact that the qualities required in teachers to make them successful teachers of reading are qualities that disqualify them as successful teachers of penmanship? Thus it might be said that teachers with a well-developed sense of relative values will emphasize reading and subordinate penmanship, whereas teachers without such a sense of relative values will give relatively more attention to penmanship. Were this the case, a negative r such as that obtained would result.

Again, it may be that the supervisors of these teachers had recommended that they shift the emphasis during the current year more in the direction of reading or vice versa, and that some of the teachers were able to respond to such a suggestion where other teachers were unable so to control their emphasis, owing to long established habits or the like. This, too, would tend to result in negative relationship.

3. The mean of all the r's between reading and other subjects is very low, being only .13 for the rural and only .26 for the urban teachers. Evidently it is not possible with any great degree of accuracy to estimate a teacher's efficiency in arithmetic or other skill subjects from knowledge of his efficiency as a teacher of reading.

4. For the urban teachers, the data do not reveal any tendency toward negative relationship between reading and penmanship. This failure to corroborate the rural findings in this matter discounts to some extent any attempt to explain the reason for the negative r as something inherent in the constitution of teachers themselves, except so far as such inherent qualities may manifest themselves in situations which are not necessarily present in all environments.

5. While the urban data fail to corroborate the negative r for the rural data, both are agreed that reading correlates less positively with penmanship than with any other of the four subjects.

6. The highest single r is between reading and arithmetic for the urban teachers. This particular relationship is next to the lowest in the rural situation.

7. The correlation coefficients for the urban teachers average twice the size of the coefficients for the rural teachers. This may be due to inequalities in the training of the teachers or inequalities in the amount or quality of supervision given the rural teachers in the different subjects. Certainly it is somewhat surprising to find the lowest r's for the data which are supposedly more heterogeneous.

The second approach for the interpretation of the above r's is through Kelley's [9] k or Bailor's [10] Predictive Index. The latter may be computed directly or by means of the formula:

$$\text{Predictive Index} = 1.0 - k$$

Thus, those already familiar with k and its meaning can think of the predictive index as the arithmetic complement of k. The advantage of the predictive index is that it increases from 0 to 1.0 with increases of r from 0 to $+1.0$ or 0 to -1.0, whereas k decreases from 1.0 to 0 with increases of r from 0 to $+1.0$ or 0 to -1.0. For this reason the predictive index is preferred to k as a basis for the interpretation of r.

An r gives directly an interpretation of the amount of correlation but not a predictive value. When r's are used as indices of prediction they lead to over-optimism as to how accurately we can predict a teacher's efficiency, say, in arithmetic, from knowledge of his efficiency as a teacher of reading. An r of 0 has a predictive index of 0 and an r of $+1.0$ or -1.0 has a predictive index of 1.0, but an r of .5 does not have a predictive index of .5. Its predictive

OBJECTIVE EFFICIENCY MEASURES

index is less than .5. Regardless of whether the r is positive or negative, the predictive index corresponding to each of the various sizes of r is as follows:

r	00	.10	.20	.30	.40	.50	.60	.70	.80	.85	.90	.95	.97	.99	1.0
PI	00	.01	.02	.05	.08	.13	.20	.29	.40	.53	.56	.69	.76	.86	1.0

When each of the r's already given is transmuted into its approximate predictive index by means of the foregoing table, it will be found that the above conclusion as to the very slight correlation found to exist between reading and other subjects is amply justified. For it is the predictive value that is the practical value of correlation coefficients.

The third approach to an interpretation of each of the above coefficients of correlation is through its probable error, usually abbreviated to PE. The PE tells us the degree of assurance we can feel as to whether a given conclusion based upon the data used in this study would be verified were similar data collected on another group of rural or urban teachers of which these teachers may be assumed to be an approximate random sampling. A high r, either positive or negative, derived from a large number of teachers makes for a desirable low PE. Thus PE varies with the size of the r and the size of the sampling of teachers. The following table will enable the reader to transmute any r from 0 to .80 into its approximate PE, and thus test the reliability of any conclusion the writer may formulate on the basis of r's presented in this study:

r	00	.05	.10	.15	.20	.25	.30	.35	.40	.45	.50	.55	.60	.65	.70	.75	.80
PE (rural)	.13	.12	.11	.11	.10	.09	.09	.08	.08	.07	.06	.06	.05	.04	.04	.03	.03
PE (urban)	.22	.21	.20	.19	.18	.17	.16	.15	.13	.12	.11	.10	.09	.08	.06	.05	.04

The size of the PE is of no particular consequence so long as the conclusions are limited to the particular group of teachers studied. The function of the PE is to limit conclusions for, say, all rural teachers on the basis of the results obtained with this sampling of rural teachers, and similarly for urban teachers. With this understanding as to the function of PE let us illustrate its application. We have already concluded that there is a negative r between efficiency in teaching reading and penmanship in the case of these rural teachers. Is this conclusion true for all rural teachers? The data do not permit us to answer this question, owing to the fact that it is not certain that these rural teachers can properly be regarded as a random sampling of rural teachers. It is more probable that they are a sampling of somewhat superior rural teachers, particularly with respect to the supervision they have received. So this must be one limitation upon any attempt to generalize conclusions for all rural teachers.

Then, are we justified in generalizing the above conclusion for somewhat superior rural teachers? Our answer is found by comparing the size of the negative r with the size of the PE of that r. The r is $-.11$. Reference to the above table shows that its approximate PE is .11. We can be practically certain that the generalization is sound provided the $-.11$ is equal to or larger than 4.4 times its PE. Its PE, namely, .11 multiplied by 4.4, gives .48. Manifestly, we cannot be practically certain that such a conclusion applies to all similar rural teachers. It is even more certain, however, that we cannot conclude with certainty that a positive r is the real truth for all similar rural teachers. The probability that the relationship is really and truly negative is greater than the probability that it is positive or zero. The scientifically correct procedure is to accept the existence of such a negative r as a tentative conclusion until it has been tested on more rural teachers. The predictive value of other r's and the reliability of other conclusions can be determined in a similar manner.

For the sake of economy of presentation, subsequent r's will not receive the attention devoted to those already presented, nor will the same care be exercised in indicating the limitations upon conclusions made necessary by knowledge of the predictive index and PE for each r. The reader is to assume, however, that they are constantly in the writer's mind. Unless the writer specifically states otherwise, the reader is to assume that all subsequent conclusions are meant to apply only to the teachers and to the data studied, and are thought of as being generalized only in the tentative sense indicated above, unless the PE in each particular case justifies more assurance.

TO WHAT EXTENT IS A TEACHER'S EFFICIENCY IN TEACHING ARITHMETIC AN INDEX OF HIS EFFICIENCY IN TEACHING OTHER SUBJECTS?

The answer to this question is given by the following coefficients, which may be interpreted as stated below:

	Reading	Spelling	Composition	Penmanship	Mean
Arithmetic (rural)....	.12	.21	.07	−.01	.10
Arithmetic (urban)....	.43	.08	.06	.46	.26

1. There is slight positive correlation between efficiency in teaching arithmetic and efficiency in teaching respectively reading, spelling and composition. This is true for both the rural and the urban teachers.

2. For the rural teachers, there is a very slight tendency for the better teachers of arithmetic to be the poorer teachers of penmanship. This is the second instance where penmanship has shown negative relationship with other subjects.

3. The urban r between penmanship and arithmetic most decidedly fails to agree with that for the rural data.

4. The highest r's are between arithmetic and reading and between arithmetic and penmanship, in the case of the urban data. Just why such obviously diverse subjects as reading and penmanship should show this similarity is something of a mystery.

5. The urban data yield a mean r that is more than twice the size of that yielded by the rural data. This conclusion has appeared twice thus far.

6. The average correlation between arithmetic and each of the other subjects is practically identical with that between reading and the other subjects. This is a matter of some surprise. Most persons would probably guess that reading would show higher correlations than arithmetic.

TO WHAT EXTENT IS A TEACHER'S EFFICIENCY IN TEACHING SPELLING AN INDEX OF HIS EFFICIENCY IN TEACHING OTHER SUBJECTS?

The coefficients of correlation which answer this question are given below and are followed by conclusions based upon them:

	Reading	Arithmetic	Composition	Penmanship	Mean
Spelling (rural).......	.23	.21	.13	−.19	.10
Spelling (urban)......	.24	.08	.13	.12	.14

1. Both rural and urban r's show very slight positive correlation between spelling and reading, arithmetic and penmanship respectively.

48   EFFICIENCY IN SUPERVISION AND TEACHING

2. For the rural teachers, there is slight negative correlation between spelling and penmanship. This is the third instance of negative correlation between penmanship and other subjects.

3. For the urban teachers, the r between spelling and penmanship is quite low, but it is not negative.

4. The highest single r is between spelling and reading.

5. The urban data yield a mean of the r's that is barely higher than that for the rural data. Thus far there has been no exception to the conclusion that the urban efficiency measures are more closely related than the rural efficiency measures.

6. The mean correlation between spelling and the other subjects is only about half as much as between reading or arithmetic and other subjects.

TO WHAT EXTENT IS A TEACHER'S EFFICIENCY IN TEACHING COMPOSITION AN INDEX OF HIS EFFICIENCY IN TEACHING OTHER SUBJECTS?

The coefficients of correlations and the conclusions relevant to this question are given below:

	Reading	Arithmetic	Spelling	Penmanship	Mean
Composition (rural)...	.28	.07	.13	.32	.20
Composition (urban)..	.22	.06	.13	.28	.17

1. Both the rural and urban r's show a slight positive correlation between composition and each of the other subjects.

2. Composition is the only subject thus far to show uniformly positive correlation between all subjects for both rural and urban data.

3. Composition is also distinctive in that the size of the r's is strikingly uniform for both rural and urban data. There are no strikingly high or strikingly low r's between any subjects.

4. Composition is also distinctive in that there is almost perfect agreement between the r's for the rural and the urban data.

5. The lowest correlation is between composition and arithmetic. The dissimilarity between composition ability and arithmetical ability on the part of the pupils is probably greater than between composition ability and of reading, spelling or penmanship ability. It would be interesting to determine whether those abili-

OBJECTIVE EFFICIENCY MEASURES

ties of the pupils which are loosely related are likewise loosely related for the efficiency measures of the teachers. It may well be that traits in pupils which show low correlation with each other require for that very reason relatively distinct teaching methods to develop them. It would also be interesting to determine the truth of the plausible inference that the lowest correlation between efficiency measures is found between subjects which require relatively more discreet teaching techniques.

6. The highest r is between composition and penmanship and reading respectively. Why? Perhaps those qualities of the teacher which make for success in teaching composition also make for success in teaching reading and penmanship. Were this the case we would expect to find positive correlation between reading and penmanship, but the r is negative. This discounts the foregoing explanation.

Another hypothesis is that the successful teacher of reading or of penmanship or of both multiplies the composition abilities of the pupils beyond that given through direct instruction in composition. There is some ground to believe that this hypothesis has some truth in it, particularly so far as penmanship and composition are concerned. The method of measuring the compositions of the pupils was to estimate their general merit. Probably the judges could not resist giving a somewhat higher mark to those compositions where the penmanship was excellent and lower marks to those where the penmanship was poor. The efficient teacher of penmanship would thus be given some statistical appearance of being an efficient teacher of composition. The effect of this would be to raise the correlation between composition and penmanship efficiency measures of the teachers.

The hypothesis that an improved reading ability will in and of itself tend to improve the composition ability of the pupils seems less certain, but still quite plausible. It is possible that a thorough investigation would show that those pupils who read well and much receive a contribution therefrom to their composition style, vocabulary and other elements that go to make up ability in composition.

The above hypothetical explanation of the relatively high r's between composition and reading and penmanship respectively is strengthened by the fact that spelling correlates higher with composition than does arithmetic. This is just what the hypothesis would lead us to expect since spelling bears the same contributive relation to composition that penmanship bears to composition.

7. Composition is also distinctive in that it provides the first instance thus far of a general tendency of the r's for the urban data to be lower than the r's for the rural data.

8. The mean of the r's between composition and the other subjects shows that composition correlates higher in general with other subjects than does spelling, and about the same as the correlation between reading or arithmetic and the other subjects.

TO WHAT EXTENT IS A TEACHER'S EFFICIENCY IN TEACHING PENMANSHIP AN INDEX OF HIS EFFICIENCY IN TEACHING OTHER SUBJECTS?

The coefficients of correlation and the conclusions relevant to this question are given below:

	Reading	Arithmetic	Spelling	Composition	Mean
Penmanship (rural)...	−.11	−.01	−.19	.32	.00
Penmanship (urban)...	.15	.46	.12	.28	.25

1. In the case of the rural data, penmanship shows slight negative correlation with all other subjects except composition. This negative relationship between penmanship efficiency measures and efficiency measures for other subjects is the outstanding characteristic of penmanship.

2. Penmanship is mercurial in its behavior. The negative r's for the rural data are not at all corroborated by the r's for the urban data. In the urban situation considerable emphasis was placed upon progress in penmanship. The pupils were taught to make use of penmanship scales to measure their own progress. It is possible that when teachers make a definite attempt to teach a subject well the best teachers of other subjects tend to be the best teachers of penmanship also. If this is so, it would tend to explain the positive correlation between penmanship and other subjects. At the same time it may be that when no particular effort or attention is given to penmanship the better teachers in general tend to give relatively scant attention to it. Experienced supervisors report having noticed this very thing, so the hypothesis is not a purely fantastic one. It appears plausible enough to merit

an independent investigation of just what effect emphasis has upon intercorrelations.

3. Penmanship maintains its mercurial reputation in its correlation with composition. Here the urban data and the rural data agree closely as to the nature and amount of correlation between the two subjects, namely, that it is positive in direction and small in amount.

4. The mean of all the r's for penmanship is zero for the rural data and .25 for the urban data. Thus, a teacher's efficiency in teaching penmanship is of no value whatever as a basis for predicting his efficiency in teaching other skills, provided this teacher is in a rural school. In case the teacher is in an urban school, however, its predictive value compares favorably with the predictive value of efficiency measures in other subjects.

CAN ONE PREDICT A TEACHER'S ABILITY TO TEACH A NARROW SKILL FROM KNOWLEDGE OF HIS ABILITY TO TEACH ANOTHER NARROW SKILL BETTER THAN FROM KNOWLEDGE OF HIS ABILITY TO TEACH A LESS NARROW SKILL, AND VICE VERSA?

It would be generally agreed that arithmetic fundamentals and spelling and penmanship are relatively narrow skills as compared with reading and composition. The answer to our question will be found by comparing the average size of the cross-correlations among the narrow skills with the average size of the cross-correlations among the wider skills with the average size of the cross-correlations between the narrower skills and the wider skills. The following table gives the various groups of cross-correlations and the mean r's that are to be compared:

CORRELATION AMONG NARROW SKILLS

Arithmetic with spelling (rural)	.21
Arithmetic with spelling (urban)	.08
Arithmetic with penmanship (rural)	—.01
Arithmetic with penmanship (urban)	.46
Spelling with penmanship (rural)	—.19
Spelling with penmanship (urban)	.12
Mean	.11

CORRELATION AMONG WIDER SKILLS

Reading with composition (rural)	.28
Reading with composition (urban)	.22
Mean	.25

52 EFFICIENCY IN SUPERVISION AND TEACHING

Correlation Between Narrow and Wider Skills

Reading with arithmetic (rural)	.12
Reading with arithmetic (urban)	.43
Reading with spelling (rural)	.23
Reading with spelling (urban)	.24
Reading with penmanship (rural)	—.11
Reading with penmanship (urban)	.15
Composition with arithmetic (rural)	.07
Composition with arithmetic (urban)	.06
Composition with spelling (rural)	.13
Composition with spelling (urban)	.13
Composition with penmanship (rural)	.32
Composition with penmanship (urban)	.28
Mean	.17

Assuming the division of the skills into narrow and wide as being a correct one, the foregoing table justifies the conclusions given below. Equal weight has been given to the r's based upon rural data and those based upon urban data.

1. In general, one can predict a teacher's ability to teach a narrow skill more accurately from knowledge of his ability to teach a wider skill than from knowledge of his ability to teach another narrow skill. This is shown by a comparison of the mean r of .11 with the mean r of .17. This is a difference of .06 with a PE difference of .08. This difference, as well as the two that follow, is not very reliable.

2. In general, one can predict a teacher's ability to teach a wider skill more accurately from knowledge of his ability to teach another like type of skill than from knowledge of his ability to teach a narrow skill. This is shown by a comparison of the mean r of .25 with the mean r of .17.

3. One can predict a teacher's ability to teach a wider skill from knowledge of his ability to teach a like type of skill more accurately than one can predict his ability to teach a narrow skill from knowledge of his ability to teach another narrow skill. This is shown by a comparison of the mean r of .11 with the mean r of .25.

The foregoing conclusions have peculiar interest for us because similar conclusions have been found where narrow skills on the part of pupils are correlated with other narrow skills and with more complex skills, and when complex skills have been correlated with other complex skills. The general tendency invariably has been for the complex functions to correlate more closely with other complex functions than they do with narrow functions, and for complex functions to correlate more closely among themselves than narrow functions correlate among themselves.

The reader should be careful not to infer that the general tendency manifested by the above table of coefficients holds true for every subject listed.

CHAPTER VII

CORRELATION BETWEEN EFFICIENCY MEASURES AND SUPERVISORS' ESTIMATES

TO WHAT EXTENT IS A SUPERVISOR ABLE TO JUDGE TEACHERS' EFFICIENCY IN TEACHING READING?

The actual efficiency in teaching reading comprehension, as defined in terms of the Thorndike-McCall test in reading, is the mean RAR gain made by each teacher. This is indisputably the most valid method yet devised for ascertaining the real efficiency of the teacher in teaching this subject.

In order to answer the above question it was necessary to secure some quantitative expression for the supervisor's opinion of each teacher's efficiency as a teacher of reading. This was done by asking those responsible for the supervision in the rural county to meet in conference to decide upon the rank to which each of the sixty-four teachers included in this study was entitled. Those who participated in this conference were the superintendent of the county schools, the supervising teacher of the county schools, and the attendance officer. After more than usual consideration and without knowledge of the RAR gains made by the teachers, they jointly decided upon which of the ranks from one to sixty-four should be assigned to each teacher.

The superintendent was unusually well acquainted with his teachers, because he had given a great deal of attention to supervision. The attendance officer appears to have had certain unusual professional relations to the schools, such as would make her judgment worth the consideration of the two primarily responsible for judging teachers. She was invited to the conference by the superintendent. The competence of the superintendent and supervising teacher would be considered markedly above the average of such persons throughout the country. Both have done graduate study in Teachers College, Columbia University, and have had much practical experience. Therefore, it appears entirely fair to conclude that the teachers in the rural situation were rated more accurately than is commonly done, when teachers are receiving promotion ratings. This conclusion appears to be even more justified when we consider that such accuracy as typically there may be in ratings is concealed in the three or four step scale often used by different raters with different standards of rating.

In order to make sure that the supervisors were not rating one phase of reading while the test was measuring another phase, the supervisors were specifically requested to rank the teachers for their skill as teachers of the specific phase of reading measured by a defined test. The actual test was in their hands; both had taken a course in measurement which considered this particular test; both had used it extensively, and were reasonably familiar with the literature of criticism of this test as to what it measures. The study by Gates has shown that it measures depth or power of comprehension, which is that phase of silent reading that educators consider to be the most significant phase and which is generally in their mind when they speak of silent reading.

Technically, the product-moment coefficient of correlation resulting from a series of ranks correlated with a series of non-rank mean RAR gains should be multiplied by 1.0233. The effect of using this multiplier would alter the obtained r's so slightly in view of their unreliability that the original r's given below have not been altered.

Efficiency in teaching reading with estimated efficiency (rural) 27
Efficiency in teaching reading with estimated efficiency (urban) . . . . —.36

The size of the r's is startling. Assuming the validity of the measure of efficiency here used, they mean that, for all practical purposes, the combined judgments of these successful, highly trained, experienced and keenly interested supervisors are just about worthless as an index of the real efficiency of teachers of reading. It does not necessarily follow that these supervisors could not judge reading in some other sense; but we shall leave it to the reader to decide whether it is probable that the supervisors would be any more able to judge efficiency in any other phase of reading.

WHAT IS THE CORRELATION BETWEEN ABILITY TO TEACH SKILLS AND ESTIMATED ABILITY TO TEACH EVERYTHING EXCEPT CHARACTER?

The composite of the mean AR gains for all subjects will be used as the measure of each teacher's ability to teach the skills. The estimated ability to teach everything except character is the rank given each teacher in this respect by the supervisors previously mentioned. The content of everything—except character—includes what intelligent supervisors consider it to mean. It certainly covers reading, arithmetic, spelling, composition, penmanship, geography, history, music, art, etc., or such phases of these as they judged to be non-character phases. Thus this ranking covers, in part surely, the content of the composite AR gain. The method of assigning rankings and of computing coefficients of correlation duplicates that just given for reading.

The coefficients of correlation are:

Composite efficiency in teaching skills with estimated efficiency in teaching everything except character (rural).................. .33
Composite efficiency in teaching skills with estimated efficiency in teaching everything except character (urban)................ —.25

These r's may mean either of two things. First, they may mean that there is little correlation between real ability in teaching the skills and real ability to teach the total of what the teacher teaches minus character. If this meaning is the correct one, a corollary of it is that it is going to be a laborious task to secure an approximate measure of a teacher's efficiency in teaching even the skills and information, not to mention the still more difficult task of measuring a teacher's efficiency in building character.

Fortunately a second meaning is more probably true, namely, that we do not have even an approximately accurate estimate of the ability of the teacher to teach everything except character. It is not possible to have any confidence in the accuracy of the subjective ranking of teacher on any teaching function, after the supervisors failed so completely to designate the superior and inferior teachers of reading. Confidence is even more shaken when we see that the correlation between efficiency in teaching reading and estimates of that identical thing is lower than between the composite efficiency in teaching skills and estimates of a somewhat different group of abilities.

EFFICIENCY MEASURES

This last statement might be criticised on the ground that supervisors are unaccustomed to rate teachers on a narrow single subject such as reading. In reply, it can be stated that:

1. Silent reading and its ramifications constitute the larger part of what the elementary school teaches to children.
2. Improvement in silent reading spreads to geography, history, etc.
3. Supervisors are supposed to be able to judge such an important factor as silent reading.

In both instances thus far there has been a very slight positive r for the rural teachers, and a very slight negative r for the urban teachers.

WHAT IS THE CORRELATION BETWEEN ABILITY TO TEACH SKILLS AND ESTIMATED ABILITY TO BUILD CHARACTER?

The supervisors ranked the teachers according to their opinion of the ability of the teachers as character builders in the same way that they ranked them for ability as teachers of reading or of everything except character. The above question is answered by the following coefficients:

Composite efficiency in teaching skills with estimated efficiency in character building (rural)..	.32
Composite efficiency in teaching skills with estimated efficiency in character building (urban)	—.12

It is interesting to learn that composite efficiency in teaching skills is just as accurate an index of ability to build character as it is of ability to teach everything except character. Both the rural and urban supervisors are substantially agreed that the moulding of purposes is just as closely related to the inculcation of skills as the inculcation of skills is related to the inculcation of knowledge and skills. Whether the supervisors are correct depends upon the amount of validity we assume their rankings of the teachers to have. It seems probable that the rankings of the urban supervisor have less than just no validity, whereas the rankings by the rural supervisors have a small amount of validity.

WHAT IS THE CORRELATION BETWEEN ABILITY TO TEACH SKILLS AND ESTIMATED ABILITY TO TEACH IN GENERAL?

The ranking given by the supervisors on ability to build character and that on ability to teach everything except character were averaged to get a ranking on ability to teach in general. This was then correlated with the composite efficiency measure. The coefficients follow:

Composite efficiency in teaching skills with estimated efficiency in general (rural).. .32
Composite efficiency in teaching skills with estimated efficiency in general (urban) .... —.26

The size and direction of these r's for both rural and urban data correspond remarkably to the size and direction of those given in the two preceding tables. In fact all the correlations reported between efficiency measures based on tests and efficiency measures based on supervisory estimates have shown a like correspondence. The reason for this similarity will become clear when we report the intercorrelations between supervisory estimates of ability to teach reading, character and everything except character.

WHAT ARE THE INTERCORRELATIONS BETWEEN ESTIMATES OF TEACHERS' ABILITY TO TEACH READING, TEACH EVERYTHING EXCEPT CHARACTER AND BUILD CHARACTER?

Since all the estimates made by the supervisors are in rank form, the desired intercorrelations were computed according to the formula for *rho* rather than in accordance with the formula for the product-moment r. These two coefficients, namely *rho* and r, are of almost identical size and are interpreted in identical manner. The reader may think of *rho* as r. The *rho*'s so computed follow. They have been computed for the more reliable rural estimates only:

Estimated ability to teach reading with estimated ability to teach everything except character (rural)......................... .9906
Estimated ability to teach reading with estimated ability to build character (rural) .... .98893
Estimated ability to teach everything except character with estimated ability to build character (rural)............................ .98894

Comment was made in a preceding section about the striking way in which the size and direction of the coefficients corroborated each other. The above *rho*'s make the reason for this evident. The supervisors gave practically the same ranking to a teacher in each of reading, everything except character, and character. Consequently and inevitably, any one series of rankings correlates about the same with composite efficiency according to the tests as does any other series of rankings.

TABLE III
RHO'S BETWEEN SUPERVISORS' RANKINGS OF TEACHERS' ABILITY TO TEACH (1) COMPREHENSION IN READING, (2) EVERYTHING EXCEPT CHARACTER, AND (3) CHARACTER

Supervisor	(1) and (2)	(1) and (3)	(2) and (3)
A	.8770	.7990	.9030
B	.9602	.8707	.8294
C	.8286	.7578	.8136
D	.8536	.5248	.7278
E	.8316	.7866	.7038
F	.9865	.9682	.9720
G	.8527	.7639	.6903
Average	.8843	.7815	.8057

The foregoing finding is of such tremendous significance that it seemed advisable to check it by securing ratings from other supervisors of other teachers. Accordingly, seven experienced supervisors were each requested to use the same procedure as that used by the supervisors in this study in rating twenty teachers. Table III shows the correlations (rho's) secured from each of these supervisors together with the average of each column of rho's. Though the correlations are not as high as those secured from the ratings of the rural supervisors, they are all positive and high.

It cannot well be argued that the supervisors rated the teachings in one trait and then to save themselves trouble gave the teacher about the same ratings in other traits. The supervisors made an earnest and interested attempt to give their best possible rankings. They appreciated the importance of what they were doing. They knew that it was to be used to study the accuracy of their estimates. Furthermore, there are evidences of real discrimination in their rankings. Occasionally some teacher received a substantially different rank in the different traits. There is reason to believe that the rankings given represented the carefully considered opinion which the supervisors had of the teachers in the three different aspects of their work. The similarity of the three series of rankings may be due to what Professor Thorndike calls the halo effect, but Thorndike has not disputed the psychological genuineness of this halo effect.

The foregoing *rho*'s do not permit us to conclude with certainty that teachers who are skillful in teaching measurable traits tend to be skillful teachers of character also. The data merely reveal what the supervisors in this study think about this question. It is possible that what supervisors think about teachers is far from being identical with what teachers really are.

WHAT IS THE ESTIMATE OF COMPETENT JUDGES AS TO THE SIZE AND DIRECTION OF CERTAIN EFFICIENCY CORRELATIONS ALREADY REPORTED?

The answer to this question has been sought in order to throw additional light upon the dependability of subjective opinion as a basis for determining the actual efficiency of teachers. To this end approximately one hundred students of education in Teachers College, Columbia University, were asked to estimate what correlations were found for the rural data. Table IV shows under the appropriate headings the number of individuals estimating the size and direction of the r for the heading in question to be as shown in the first column. Thus, five individuals estimated the r to be .9 between efficiency in teaching reading with efficiency in teaching arithmetic. Four individuals estimated the r to be nearest to 1.0 between supervisors' estimates of teachers' ability to build character and their estimate of teachers' ability to teach everything except character. The heavier type under each heading indicates the size of the r shown in the first column that was actually obtained. A study of this table leads to the following conclusions:

1. There is great divergence of opinion as to the amount of correlation that actually exists between any two of the items listed. This emphasizes the original need for an investigation of the actual amount of correlation, since the importance of correct knowledge with respect to this matter is obvious. Some of the divergence can be accounted for as due to lack of thorough experience in interpreting coefficients of correlation on the part of some of the judges. It is probable that the amount of the allowance that must be made for this is small. The class from which

TABLE IV
Various Intercorrelations Between Teaching Efficiency Measures and Supervisory Rankings of Teacher Efficiency, Together with Estimates of What These Correlations Are

r	Read. Arith.	Read. Spell.	Read. Comp.	Read. Pen.	Read. Est. Read.	Read. Est. Char.	Comp. Est. All Except Char.	Comp. Est. All Except Char.	Est. Char.
1.0...	....	3	5	....	....	1	2	4
.9...	5	6	12	....	2	1	9	9
.8...	15	20	23	....	14	8	8	17
.7...	8	27	13	1	10	6	15	7
.6...	10	19	14	6	7	9	13	8
.5...	35	8	21	11	31	21	25	15
.4...	5	10	10	8	13	12	10	7
.3...	9	3	2	9	9	7	3	12
.2...	4	1	....	9	4	9	8	8
.1...	4	1	1	2	3	5	3	2
0...	6	4	....	42	3	17	3	10
− .1...	....	....	....	2	....	1	....	....
− .2...	....	....	....	1	3	1	1	....
− .3...	....	....	....	2	....	....	....	1
− .4...	....	1	....	1	....	....	....	....
− .5...	....	2	....	1	1	1	1	1
− .6...	....	....	....	1	....	....	....	....
− .7...	....	....	....	1	....	....	....	....
− .8...	....	....	....	....	....	1	....	....
− .9...	....	....	....	....	1	....	....	....
−1.0...	....	....	....	5	....	1	....	....

these estimates were secured had studied in a graduate course in measurement for almost a year. Furthermore, the meaning of r was carefully explained before the estimates were asked for.

2. The judges differed most as to the amount of correlation that exists between composite ability to teach skills as measured by tests and supervisory rankings as to ability to build character. This is where we would expect the greatest difference of opinion to exist, because this estimate registers the effects of a controversy that exists concerning the merits and demerits of the project method in education.

3. There is very wide divergence of opinion as to the correlation between tested efficiency in teaching reading and estimated efficiency in teaching reading. It is difficult to account for this relatively large variability. Possibly this also reflects the results of one of our modern educational controversies. There were doubtless those in the group of judges who have gained respect for the accuracy of reading tests but have lost their respect for the accuracy of supervisory opinion. This group would react in the direction of a high negative r. On the other hand, there were other members of the group who have either gained or maintained respect for the accuracy of both measures or else were deceived by the apparent similarity between the two things being correlated.

4. There is also wide divergence of opinion concerning the r between reading and penmanship. Thus penmanship maintains the reputation gained earlier in this study of being the most erratic item studied. Within the last few years the status of penmanship in the schools and in the esteem of educators has undergone a radical change. This change has been subtly facilitated by correlation studies which have shown that penmanship fails to correlate with other abilities or with intelligence tests in the conventional manner. This decline of penmanship has not yet reached a point of equilibrium or else has not been long enough in a condition of equilibrium to cause to be reduced to a minimum the variability of educational opinion concerning it. This is proposed as a hypothetical explanation of the variability of opinion concerning its correlation with reading. Its earlier behavior may also be influenced by this transitional factor as well as by the peculiar isolation of the ability in the neurons of children or the distinctive methods required to teach the skill to children.

5. The least divergence of opinion occurs in the case of reading with arithmetic and reading with composition. Even so, opinion varies all the way from about 0 to about 1.0.

6. There is, with one striking exception, a strong tendency to consider the correlations between the various items as being much higher than they really are. Perhaps this can be explained as due to the strong emphasis that has been given in recent educational literature to the existence of positive correlation between desirable traits. The writer confesses to being surprised at the small amount of correlation that was found to exist between different subjects, or between subjects and supervisory estimates. The surprise was even greater at the high correlation found to exist between supervisory rankings of teachers in one trait and rankings in another trait.

7. The one hundred individuals seriously underestimated the amount of correlation between supervisory ranking of teachers according to their ability to build character and according to their ability to teach everything except character. This is particularly surprising because it is just at this point that we would have a right to expect opinion to agree most closely with fact. Failure on the part of so many competent judges to predict with approximate accuracy what the three rural supervisors would do made the writer suspect that the rural supervisors were in some way atypical. But the three series of rankings given by the seven supervisors were also much higher than the 100 estimates. One is therefore forced to conclude that the most probable inference from the above is that these same one hundred judges would act quite differently from the way in which they think they would act if they were called upon to give similar rankings for real teachers whom they were supervising.

8. As usual penmanship distinguished itself by the peculiarity of its behavior. Here there is closer than usual agreement between fact and opinion. The model correlation, *i.e.*, the most frequent r, according to opinion, is 0. The r of fact is only .1 removed from this mode.

9. Practically every conclusion formulated thus far has been unfavorable for subjective opinion as a method of measuring any fact which objectively exists. The reader should not therefore infer that the writer does not fully subscribe to the position taken by McCall. In a paper as yet unpublished he says: "The net effect

of Rugg's classic analysis of the results secured from the use of the Scott Rating Scale is to cast grave suspicion upon the accuracy of all subjective measurements of facts which have an independent existence outside the mental life of the measurer. But it should not be forgotten that there are a multitude of extremely significant facts that exist within the mental life of the measurer which he can subjectively measure and overtly report with an accuracy far exceeding that of most objective tests." The final interpretation given here may go beyond the position taken by McCall and record a surprising triumph for the accuracy of the central tendency of subjective measurements of facts which have an existence independent of the mental life of the measurer. While the average opinion of one hundred judges is badly in error as to the absolute amount of correlation that actually exists between different items, it is surprisingly correct as to the relative amounts of correlation. The reader can see this best if he will turn to Table IV and draw straight lines connecting all the figures in heavy type, and then draw similar lines connecting the modal frequency under each heading. The parallelism of the two curves thus constructed will be striking, especially within that portion of the table where data are most comparable.

TO WHAT EXTENT IS PROFESSIONAL KNOWLEDGE AN INDEX OF TEACHING EFFICIENCY?

It is very fortunate that just as this study was nearing completion the Steele-Herring test of professional information was also nearing completion. In the process of constructing this test Miss Roxanna Steele applied it to most of the rural teachers included in this study, and furnished the total scores on both forms of the test. The two scores for each teacher were combined into a single score representing a very thorough and quite reliable sampling of each teacher's professional information.

The next step was to compute the correlation between these series of total scores and the series of composite efficiency scores for these teachers. This should give about the best obtainable measure of whether or not the teacher who knows the most about modern educational ideas, theories, practices and the like is the one who is most skillful in making actual changes in children such as are measured by the tests used. This is a vital question in the training of teachers, for a great amount of time is given in our normal schools to inculcating modern educational ideas and knowledge of its principles and practices. Does this knowledge function?

Correlation between knowledge and actual changes made in children.. .046

This is so startlingly low that one immediately seeks for some explanation other than the probable one, namely, that actual efficiency in teaching is negligibly correlated with how much the teacher knows about educational ideas and practices. Or, stated more exactly, such differences in knowledge as exist among rural teachers are worthless if their value is to be judged by their contribution to desirable changes in children as measured by the tests used in this study. Of course, not all desirable changes made in these rural children were measured. But it is reasonable to conclude that if differences in knowledge are significant their significance would appear in some or all of the subjects that were measured.

It cannot reasonably be claimed that the test of professional knowledge is an inferior test. The test was prepared with unusual care. In preparing it the author had the collaboration of one expert in test construction and the close supervision of another. The total testing time was two hours. The test is very representative, in that it covers many fields of educational thought. A great number of the test items called for answers to questions concerning practical processes of teaching in general and practical processes of teaching different subjects. Many of the questions deal with the proper method of teaching the very subjects covered in this study. There is no doubt that we are faced here with a problem of significance for teacher training, and one that should be exhaustively studied forthwith. The Steele-Herring test of professional information, standardized tests, and the teaching efficiency formula provide some of the instruments for the study of this problem.

The total combined score on the Steele-Herring test was also correlated with the composite of the ranking given to the teachers by the supervisors. The resulting correlation is as follows:

Correlation between knowledge and supervisor's estimate............ .407

This correlation is quite low, but still substantial enough to raise the question as to why. Evidently the professional information test favors the same teachers that are favored by supervisors when rating teachers. Must we conclude that this is evidence of the fact that both are measuring some real and desirable thing in teachers? Is this evidence that there is a fundamental defect of some sort in the formula for measuring teachers' efficiency? Another explanation is possible, namely, that supervisors tend to rate teachers high who have a ready command of educational phraseology and are fluent in the discussion of modern educational ideas. Both professional test and supervisors may be measuring this quite well and yet not be giving a real measure of efficiency.

CHAPTER VIII

CRITICISMS OF THE EFFICIENCY FORMULA

DOES THE TYPE OF SCHOOL GIVE A SPECIAL ADVANTAGE OR HANDICAP TO THE TEACHER?

To assist in answering this question there is given in Table V a distribution of the mean AR changes made by each class in each subject in each type of school, namely, one-room, two-room, three-room, and urban.

The main points brought out by Table V may be listed as follows:

1. In general, the largest amount of AR change that occurs is in reading. Next in order in this respect comes penmanship. Arithmetic is third, composition fourth, and spelling last. Probably most of these differences are due to the decision of the teachers to emphasize certain subjects to the detriment of others.

2. In general, the mean change in AR for all types of schools is above the norm, namely zero, in all subjects. All investigations show that every measurement program is accompanied by such favorable changes. Whether this is because of the measurements themselves, or because of the increased interest of the teachers and pupils, or to more effective teaching and supervision when guided by the results of tests or a combination of these, it is impossible to say.

3. Reading, composition and penmanship AR changes are extremely variable, whereas the AR changes for arithmetic and spelling, and particularly spelling, showed much less variability. Only a very small part of this variability can be accounted for as due to errors of measurement, hence most of it must be due to differences of emphasis on the part of different teachers or differences in teaching skill. It may be that all teachers teach spelling with about equal effectiveness. Perhaps the process for teaching it is so routine and so well standardized that all teachers can master and use the process with about equal success, whereas the process

TABLE V. DISTRIBUTION OF MEAN AR CHANGES FOR EACH CLASS, EACH

AR Changes

	-20 -19	-18 -17	-16 -15	-14 -13	-12 -11	-10 -9	-8 -7	-6 -5	-4 -3	-2 -1	0 1	2 3
READING												
1-room	....	....	....	....	....	....	....	1	2	1	3	3
2-room	....	....	....	....	1	....	....	....	....	....	....	1
3-room	....	....	....	....	....	....	....	....	....	....	1	....
Urban	....	....	....	....	....	....	....	....	....	....	....	2
Total	....	....	....	....	1	....	....	1	2	1	4	6
ARITHMETIC												
1-room	....	....	....	....	....	....	....	1	1	2	5	5
2-room	....	....	....	....	....	....	....	1	....	1	....	....
3-room	....	....	....	....	....	1	....	....	....	....	1	3
Urban	....	....	....	....	....	....	....	1	9	1	3	5
Total	....	....	....	....	....	1	....	3	10	4	9	11
SPELLING												
1-room	....	....	....	....	....	....	....	1	2	9	12	8
2-room	....	....	....	....	....	1	....	....	2	2	3	1
3-room	....	....	....	....	....	....	....	....	1	6	6	3
Urban	....	....	....	....	....	....	....	2	6	5	3	2
Total	....	....	....	....	....	1	....	3	12	22	24	14
COMPOSITION												
1-room	....	1	....	1	....	....	2	2	3	8	1	7
2-room	....	....	....	1	....	....	2	1	2	1	....	....
3-room	....	....	....	....	....	....	....	1	1	1	1	....
Urban	....	1	2	....	....	....	4	2	....	....	2	1
Total	....	2	2	2	....	....	8	6	6	10	4	8
PENMANSHIP												
1-room	....	....	....	....	....	....	....	....	....	1	....	4
2-room	....	....	....	....	....	....	....	....	1	....	1	2
3-room	....	....	....	....	....	....	....	....	2	....	1	1
Urban	1	....	....	2	....	1	2	....	1	....	1	1
Total	1	....	....	2	....	1	2	....	4	1	3	8

Composite AR Change

	-6 -2	-3 -1	0 2	3 5	6 8	9 11	12 14	15 17	18 20
1-room	1	1	....	4	....	4	4	3	9
2-room	....	1	....	2	....	2	....	....	2
3-room	....	....	....	....	1	1	....	4	1
Urban	....	1	1	5	2	2	1	1	2
Total	1	3	1	11	3	9	5	8	14

SUBJECT AND EACH TYPE OF SCHOOL, AND TOTAL FOR ALL TYPES

4–6	6–7	8–9	10–11	12–13	14–15	16–17	18–19	20–21	22–23	24–25	26–27	28–29	Mean
5	2	5	1	1	5	3	1	....	1	....	....	....	8.1
1	2	2	1	1	....	1	1	....	1	1	....	1	11.9
2	1	2	....	2	2	2	1	2	....	....	....	1	13.5
3	1	1	2	4	5	2	1	....	....	....	....	....	11.4
11	6	11	6	9	9	7	3	2	2	1	....	2	10.2
7	6	4	3	....	....	....	....	....	....	....	....	....	4.6
7	1	3	....	1	....	....	....	....	....	....	....	....	6.4
3	5	2	....	1	....	....	....	....	....	....	....	....	5.3
1	....	1	....	....	1	....	....	....	....	....	....	....	0.6
18	12	10	3	2	1	....	....	....	....	....	....	....	3.9
....	1	....	....	....	....	....	....	....	....	....	....	....	0.6
3	1	....	1	....	....	....	....	....	....	....	....	....	1.6
2	....	....	....	....	....	....	....	....	....	....	....	....	−0.7
5	2	....	1	....	....	....	....	....	....	....	....	....	0.4
2	2	2	1	2	....	....	....	....	....	....	....	....	0.9
2	1	....	1	1	....	....	1	1	....	....	....	....	3.0
4	3	1	1	1	1	....	1	....	....	....	....	....	6.2
1	2	....	3	1	1	....	....	....	....	....	....	....	0.0
9	8	3	6	5	2	....	2	1	....	....	....	....	2.0
1	4	10	2	....	4	2	2	3	....	....	....	1	11.2
1	3	....	....	3	....	1	....	1	....	....	1	....	9.6
4	....	1	....	3	....	2	1	....	....	....	....	1	9.2
2	1	2	2	1	1	....	2	....	....	....	....	....	2.8
8	8	13	4	7	5	5	5	4	....	....	1	2	8.5

21–23	24–26	27–29	30–32	33–35	36–38	39–41	42–44	45–47	Mean
5	......	1	1	1	......	......	......	......	15.9
2	1	2	......	......	......	......	1	1	20.4
5	1	1	2	......	......	......	......	......	22.0
1	1	1	......	1	......	1	......	......	12.6
13	3	5	3	2	0	1	1	1	17.1

for teaching, say composition, reading and penmanship, is less routine and less standardized. Possibly these subjects offer greater scope for the play of native aptitudes for teaching, or else make a larger demand upon intelligence or general all-round ability. This whole subject is of sufficient importance to merit a special investigation.

4. The urban schools, as shown by the means in the last column of the table, are consistently lower than any other type of school. Does this mean that the formula for the measurement of a teacher's efficiency handicaps a teacher in urban schools?

5. The largest penmanship mean AR change was made by one-room schools. The second largest was made by two-room schools, while the least change was made by three-room schools.

6. The largest spelling mean AR change was made by two-room schools. Three-room and one-room schools each made about the same amount of change, the means being practically zero in both cases.

7. In every other subject besides spelling and penmanship there is a strong tendency for the three-room schools to be the best, two-room schools second, and one-room schools third.

8. The distribution of composite AR changes shows the three-room schools as having made the largest amount of AR change. The two-room schools rank second and the one-room schools third. This gives the best measure of the relative effectiveness of the three types of rural schools because the composite takes significance of the subject into account.

Do the foregoing facts signify that the formula for measuring teaching efficiency favors teachers in three-room schools over teachers in two-room schools, and teachers in two-room schools over teachers in one-room schools, and teachers in one-room rural schools over teachers in urban schools? Such a conclusion is not warranted by the data. The conclusion is just as tenable that the teachers in three-room schools really are more efficient than teachers in two-room, one-room and urban schools, and to just the extent shown by the data in the table. There is, in fact, reason to believe that the best teachers in a county gravitate toward the consolidated schools while the least efficient are forced to content themselves with more isolated positions.

There is some internal evidence in the table to show that the formula has been fair to all types of schools. In general we would

CRITICISM OF THE EFFICIENCY FORMULA 71

expect that the poorer teachers would be the ones who would produce gain in penmanship more than in reading and composition and that it would be the better teachers who would do the opposite thing. The teachers in the one-room schools produced more AR changes in penmanship than in reading or composition. The teachers in the three-room schools gave relatively more emphasis to reading and composition than to penmanship.

To sum up, the nature of the data available in this investigation does not enable the factor of type of school to be sufficiently isolated from the probable factor of selection of superior teachers by consolidated schools to permit a satisfactory study of the effect, if any, of type of school upon the validity of the formula for measuring teaching efficiency. But the data do present certain internal evidence which is favorable to the conclusion that the formula does not seriously penalize, if it penalizes at all, the teachers in one-room rural schools as compared with teachers in two-room or three-room schools.

Tentatively, then, we can say that three-room schools have more efficient teachers than two-room schools, which in turn have more efficient teachers than one-room schools. A final conclusion to this effect is not possible until such factors as amount of supervision given, adequacy of equipment, quality of the mentality of the pupils and the like have been isolated and studied.

It is questionable whether it would be worth while discussing further the efficiency of rural as compared with urban schools. The data from the rural and urban schools are not strictly comparable since the interval between initial and final tests was different, and since there were many other differences. Since the interval was longer for the urban teachers and since their equipment in the way of books and other facilities is considered superior, it seems difficult to avoid the conclusion that these urban teachers proved less efficient in teaching the skills as measured by the tests used than these rural teachers.

DOES THE INITIAL IQ OF THE CLASS AFFECT THE VALIDITY OF THE FORMULA FOR THE MEASUREMENT OF TEACHING EFFICIENCY?

Practically every investigation that has been made since the AR formula was developed shows that dull children tend to have higher AR's than do bright children. In fact there has been decided negative correlation between IQ and AR. This fact has led many to formulate the very reasonable conclusion that teachers of classes of dull children have a decided advantage over the teachers of relatively bright classes.

As a first step in this direction a scatter diagram was constructed for the two variables, mean IQ for each class and mean RAR gain for each class. An inspection of this diagram showed a low but positive correlation between the two. This may be interpreted as showing that low IQ classes made less rather than greater RAR gain than the brighter classes. Thus the subject of reading reverses the common expectation.

But before this rather surprising conclusion is accepted it is well to inquire whether this positive correlation is due to the operation of factors with which IQ's are associated rather than to IQ itself. Thus, for example, it may be that the one-room schools have lower IQ classes and, at the same time, less efficient teachers than those possessed by the two- and three-room schools. Should this be the case, the result would be a positive correlation between mean IQ and mean RAR gain without there being any necessary causal relation between IQ and gain.

The following mean of the IQ's for the one-room, two-room and three-room schools shows that the children who go to two-room schools are more intelligent than the children who go to one-room schools, and that those who go to three-room schools are more intelligent than those who go to two-room schools:

	One-room	Two-room	Three-room
Mean Intelligence Quotient	93.8	94.5	103.6
Probable Error of Mean	.52	.67	.54

The PE of a mean is interpreted in the same way as a PE of an r. That is, one can be practically certain that the true mean for all one-room schools similar to those in the rural situation studied does not differ from the obtained mean of 103.6 by more than 4.4 times the PE of that mean, namely, .54. The conclusion is therefore justified that the mean IQ of three-room schools is reliably higher than for two-room or one-room schools, and that while the mean IQ for two-room schools is higher than for one-room schools one cannot be practically certain that this is true for all two-room schools in the country.

CRITICISM OF THE EFFICIENCY FORMULA

Of course no reader will make the mistake of thinking that the above figures mean that the effect of consolidating schools is to raise the Intelligence Quotients of the children who attend them. It is much more probable that consolidation takes place first in those communities where the native intelligence of parents and therefore children is relatively higher than where it does not take place, or else that parents of higher native intelligence move with their more gifted children to those communities which have such consolidation.

This conclusion that one-room schools tend to have children of lower intelligence than consolidated schools is so significant that the reader should be cautioned against fully accepting it. The improbable may really be true, namely, that consolidating schools does raise the intelligence of the children, especially that kind of intelligence which is measured by the National Intelligence Test used in this study. This test contains elements the mastery of which may depend upon the type of schooling the child has had. In case consolidating schools attracted to them the better teachers, it is conceivable that the entire difference found between the mean IQ for the three-room and one-room schools may be due to this superior instruction. Much more thorough testing by many types of intelligence tests is required before it is possible to formulate a final conclusion relative to this matter.

All this means that the observed positive correlation between mean and class IQ's and mean RAR gains may be due to high IQ classes finding it easier to increase their RAR gains than do low IQ classes, or it may be due, instead, to the gravitation of the more efficient teachers to the consolidated schools. The latter would produce positive correlation between IQ and RAR gain even though the teaching efficiency formula gave an exactly equal chance to classes or pupils of different IQ's.

Thus, the foregoing approach to the question raised at the beginning, though it yields interesting incidental information, does not give a certain answer to the question raised. Consequently, scatter diagrams were not constructed to show the relationship between IQ and all the other AR gains available.

At this juncture it was decided to construct a contingency table showing the relationship between IQ and RAR gain, not by classes as wholes but by individual pupils. Table VI is such a contingency table.

TABLE VI
Correlation Between Pupil IQ and Pupil RAR Gain in One-, Two- and Three-Room Rural Schools

	−35	−30	−25	−20	−15	−10	−5	0	5	10	15	20	25	30	35	40	45	50	55	60	65	Mean
135....	+			1	1			3	1	2	4	3	3	1								13.8
125....								5	1	9	4	8	10	5	4	3	3	1	1		1	20.8
115....				2		3	5	9	13	12	10	8	8	5	2	1	2	2				15.3
105....				1	5	10	13	10	22	29	15	21	7	8	4	3		3		1	1	13.8
95....			1	2	6	14	8	21	19	25	21	16	17	8	5	3	1	2	2	2		13.9
85....		1	1		8	12	17	23	24	23	14	18	10	3	3	4						9.6
75....				1	3	2	6	21	14	9	14	10	8	5		6				1		8.5
65....			2	1		3	3	5	4	5	3	2	4	2	1		1					5.3
55....	1				1	2	2		1	2					1							−4.0

Table VI enables us to state the following conclusions:

1. Very low IQ pupils tended to make RAR gains of less than zero. The lowest RAR gain made by any pupil was made by a pupil in this lowest IQ level, namely, 55 or below. No pupil in this IQ group made one of the higher RAR gains.

2. There is a steady tendency for the RAR gains to increase with increases in the size of the IQ of the pupils. This table thus corroborates the evidence of the scatter diagram previously referred to. Some corroboration would be expected since these same general data were the source of both.

3. The steady tendency for increases in IQ to be marked by increases in RAR gains continues until pupils with IQ's of 135 or over are reached. Here the trend turns toward less RAR gains than the IQ group immediately preceding.

4. This table gives no support to the current view that it is more difficult for high IQ pupils to make AR gains than for dull pupils. In fact, it supports quite the contrary view.

5. There is great variability in the RAR gains made by pupils of the same IQ group. There are some quite gifted children whose RAR goes backward during the year, just as there are some rather low IQ pupils who make large RAR gains. Errors in the measurement of individual pupils operate to make the obtained variability somewhat greater than the true variability for this same group, but there will be great variability left when proper allowance has been made for the amount of this error.

And yet, after all, Table VI does not permit the conclusion that

CRITICISM OF THE EFFICIENCY FORMULA 75

relatively larger RAR gains were made by high IQ's than lower IQ's because of differences in IQ *per se,* and thus because the teaching efficiency formula favors high IQ's and consequently teachers teaching bright pupils. It may well be, as previously stated, that high IQ's happen to be in schools where superior teachers happen to gravitate.

Since it was predictable in advance of the construction of this table that it would corroborate the conclusion from the scatter diagram and, like it, lead to an *impasse* so far as any conclusions can be drawn as to the effect of differences of IQ upon the validity of the teaching efficiency formula, the reader is probably asking why the table was constructed at all. Some of the incidental values that have come from the construction of the table are indicated in the conclusions given above. An additional value of no small significance is to have available frequency distributions of RAR gains by separate IQ groups for rural pupils. Formerly a teacher of a rural class might compute an RAR gain for a pupil, with an IQ between 95 and 105, and find it to be 5. Then she might ask her supervisor whether this were a large or a small gain. Without such information as this table gives it would be quite difficult for a supervisor to answer the question. This table shows that rural teachers have in six months produced much greater gains and also much less than this and just how many children made each gain.

But there is one point brought out by this table which is not revealed by the scatter diagram and which may have a significant and interpretable bearing upon our original question. Why do the very high IQ's reverse the trend of positive correlation?

Could this be because these very high IQ's happen to be in one-room schools where the poorer teachers are more likely to be found? The number of pupils with IQ's of 130 or over who were located in the different types of schools are as follows: One-room schools, 8; two-room schools, 8; three-room schools, 21. Hence, some other explanation for this reversal of correlational trend must be sought. Parenthetically, it might be added that the inclusion of IQ's below 135 does not alter the fact of a reversal of the positive correlation trend.

Could the reversal of the trend be due to high IQ's reaching the limits of test or curriculum or both? Only fourteen of the thirty-seven IQ's of 130 or over have mental ages below 14 years,

0 months. The other twenty-three pupils have begun to reach the limits of the curriculum or attain the point beyond which it is no longer profitable for the growth in the function tested to keep pace with the growth in intelligence, or no longer possible for it to do so because the schools do not provide the proper environment. The mean RAR gain for the fourteen high IQ pupils with mental ages below fourteen years is 24.6, which is larger than the mean RAR gain made by any IQ group. Had this group of high IQ's only been used, there would have been no reversal of the correlation trend. We may contrast with this mean of 24.6 a mean of 12.8 made by the twenty-three high IQ's whose mental ages are fourteen years or over.

There is a possible fallacy in the foregoing conclusion that there is no reversal of the positive correlation trend provided high IQ's not reaching the limits are used. It may be that there are pupils in the preceding IQ group 125-129 inclusive who are also reaching the limits. These should be eliminated before a mean can be computed which is strictly comparable to the mean of 24.6. When this is done, sixteen pupils are left. Their mean RAR gain is 20.4. So, even when means are made strictly comparable, the conclusion holds that the use of the high IQ's who are not reaching the limits continues the positive correlation pictured by distributions for IQ groups below.

Since in the long run there will be a greater percentage of mental ages that are reaching the limits of the curriculum among the high IQ group than among lower IQ groups, we have here some real evidence that the teaching efficiency formula discriminates in this regard against the teacher who is teaching a relatively bright class in the upper grades. Note, however, that it is not the teacher of bright children that is placed at a disadvantage, but the teacher of bright children in the upper grades, or the teacher of upper grades who has a considerable number of bright children in his class.

There are certain qualifications that should be placed upon the foregoing conclusion. Objective, standard tests are being used more and more to group pupils into classes on the basis of mental or educational age. If this were done in a thoroughgoing manner, it might very well happen that dull children would be reaching the limits just as frequently as bright children. This would tend to remove the handicap of an upper grade teacher with bright children in his class, for if the children are so bright that their mental

CRITICISM OF THE EFFICIENCY FORMULA 77

level is beyond the work of the eighth grade, these children would be in high school instead, where they would not be a drag upon the teaching efficiency formula.

This discussion has been proceeding on the assumption that it is just as serious for a teacher's efficiency measure for his dull pupils to reach the limits as for his bright children to do so. This study provides enough data to determine whether this assumption is a true one, but it is better not to raise too many issues at once.

To sum up the net effect of our search for an answer to the original question: We have found that there is positive correlation between IQ and RAR gain, but we have been unable to show that this is due either wholly or in part to differential effects of different IQ's. But in searching for an answer to the original question we have discovered a factor other than IQ, namely, reaching the limits of the curriculum which conditions the fairness of the teaching efficiency formula. We have shown that this is a conditioning factor when associated with high IQ's, and have inferred, though we have not yet established, that it is also a factor when associated with low or average IQ's. For the time being it is well to accept the conclusion even when associated with high IQ's as a tentative one only. The number of pupils studied is small, and their distribution among the different classes is not exactly the same for the 14 high IQ's and the 23 high IQ's. It is possible that the 14 high IQ's had the advantage of somewhat better teachers than the others.

It is now clear that the effect of IQ *per se* upon the validity of the teaching efficiency formula cannot be investigated unless some method can be employed which equates the teacher efficiency factor. This is not an impossible situation, for we are not quite in the position of one who would investigate the validity of the teaching efficiency formula, and before this can be done we must have a measure for the teacher which is entirely valid. One way of escape would be the experimental, namely, to have the same teacher teach a class of low, average and high IQ at the same time, or in succession or in rotation. Unfortunately, this best way out must be left for another dissertation to follow.

A second way out is to determine the correlation between IQ and RAR gain within the same identical class under one teacher. This equates the teacher factor. In case this yields a positive correlation, the accumulation of evidence pointing in this direction becomes important enough to merit a highly probable conclusion that it is easier for high IQ pupils to make large RAR gains than for low or average IQ pupils to do so. An assumption involved in such a conclusion, in this event, is that what is true within any given class is true from class to class. If there is a positive correlation within the class of mixed low, average and high IQ's, we cannot be absolutely sure that a teacher who has a separate class composed of relatively high IQ's will derive the expected advantage from their IQ's. However, this assumption is sufficiently plausible and probable, so that it justifies the effort to find out what the correlation is within a class.

But here a difficulty is encountered owing to the small number of pupils in each class. In the first place, the labor of calculating a separate coefficient for each class would be very great, and in the second place many of the r's so computed would not be very reliable. The method of what, for want of a better name, may be called fused correlation has been devised to overcome both of these difficulties at one stroke.

The method of fused correlation is essentially the method of composite photography. It is a method of superimposing the scatter diagram for one class upon the scatter diagram for another class, and of continuing this process until the scatter diagrams for all the classes have been fused into a single diagram yielding a single product-moment coefficient of correlation of practically the same size as would be found if separate r's were computed for each class and then all were averaged together, weighting each according to the number of pupils in the class from which it was derived. Fused correlation is appropriate in any situation where it would be appropriate to average the r's determined separately for each class.

The first step in the process of constructing the fused scatter diagram was to construct a table for converting the two variables, namely IQ and RAR gain, into numbers from 1 to 10 or more for each variable. On page 79 is an abbreviated illustration of such a table for two classes, one composed of pupils of relatively low and average IQ's making relatively small RAR gains, and another composed of pupils of relatively high IQ's making slightly higher and more widely varying RAR gains.

The data for all classes were forced into a range of 1 to 15

CRITICISM OF THE EFFICIENCY FORMULA

for IQ and 1 to 10 for reading. Whatever range was selected was kept constant for that subject for all classes.

Range of IQ	90	92	94	96	98	100	102	104	106	108	110	112	114	116	118	120	122
Lower IQ class	1	2	3	4	5	6	7	8	9	10	11	12	13	14	15	..	..
Higher IQ class	..	..	1	2	3	4	5	6	7	8	9	10	11	12	13	14	15

Range of RAR gain	-5	-4	-3	-2	-1	0	1	2	3	4	5	6	7	8	9	10	11	12	13
Lower IQ class	..	1	2	3	4	5	6	7	8	9	10	..	..	..	..	..	..	..	..
Higher IQ class	1	..	2	..	3	..	4	..	5	..	6	..	7	..	8	..	9	..	10

The second step was to construct a scatter diagram, where the two variables are not IQ and RAR gain but the numbers 1, 2, 3, 4, etc., for each. Assume the first pupil in the lower IQ class to have an IQ of 104 and an RAR gain of 0. Then this pupil was represented by a point in the scatter diagram of 8 for the IQ variable and 5 for the RAR variable. Assume a pupil in the higher IQ class to have an IQ of 116 and an RAR gain of -1. Then this pupil was plotted in the same scatter diagram as 12 and 3 respectively. The first pupil would tend to produce a positive drift in the scatter diagram, whereas the second pupil would tend to produce a negative drift in the scatter diagram. Other pupils in these and other classes were represented in the scatter diagram in the same way.

The third and last step was to compute the ordinary product-moment r from the fused scatter diagram.

Why were the IQ's and RAR gains converted into numerals from 1 up, 1 in each case being the lowest IQ in the class or the lowest RAR gain in the class? The purpose of this was to give statistical homogeneity to heterogeneous data and thus avoid the spurious correlation that would otherwise have resulted from composite correlation, owing to the mixing in one scatter diagram of groups varying greatly in mean IQ. Such spurious correlation would have resulted had not this conversion taken place even had the r's for all the separate classes been zero.

First the correlation was computed for one hundred and thirty-seven cases drawn in equal numbers from one-room and three-room schools with one class from the two-room schools. The correlation was between IQ and RAR gain. The r is a slight positive, being .197. Thus the fused correlation confirms earlier but less dependable indices. These rural teachers found it slightly easier to increase, or at least they succeeded better in increasing, the RAR of the bright children.

Inspection of the diagram showed that occasionally quite low IQ pupils made large RAR gains, as did average IQ pupils, whereas it was very rare for a very high IQ pupil to make a very large RAR gain. That is, there is a faint tendency toward a curvilinear relationship, such as has been noticed previously.

The second fused correlation computed was for IQ and AAR (Arithmetic Accomplishment Ratio) gain. This r is practically zero, being .017. Evidently, the relationship between IQ and possibilities for AR gain is not the same for reading and arithmetic. However, it should be noted that neither supports the prevailing conception that the teaching efficiency formula favors the teacher who has a dull class.

The third fused correlation computed was between IQ and SAR (Spelling Accomplishment Ratio) gain. This fused r is −.046. Like arithmetic, and not unlike reading, this r lends no support to the conventional view that teachers of dull classes have a special advantage over teachers of bright classes. Also, like the two preceding r's, this one is practically zero.

The fourth fused r was computed for IQ with CAR (Composition Accomplishment Ratio). This r is .042, which is, for all practical purposes, zero. Thus this correlation supports the findings just reported for other subjects.

The fifth fused r computed was for IQ with PAR (Penmanship Accomplishment Ratio). It is .126, an r of negligible size.

All of these five fused r's between IQ and mean Accomplishment Ratio gains in the various subjects point toward one main conclusion, namely, that within a given class all the varying IQ's had approximately an equal opportunity to make an improvement in their subject AR. There is a slight indication that the brighter the pupil the better his opportunity to make an increase. This is contrary to what was expected before the r's were computed and contrary to conventional belief. Also it makes more plausible the conclusion that bright classes and dull classes and consequently their teachers have equal chances to increase their efficiency scores.

In answer to the question heading this whole section, we can now say that it is probable that IQ has little or no effect upon the validity of the formula for measuring a teacher's efficiency.

In conclusion three observations may be made which may stimulate further research on this general problem. First, how is it possible to find in almost every instance that IQ and initial AR are correlated negatively, when IQ and AR gain are correlated slightly positively? There may be something in the nature of this investigation that stimulated the rural teachers to make better adaptation to the varying brightness in the classroom. Second, there is a noticeable tendency for the positive correlation between IQ and AR to be higher for those subjects in which great AR gain was made than for those subjects in which little AR gain was made. The least AR gain was made in the subjects of spelling and arithmetic, and these show the lowest correlations, in the sense of being farthest from a positive correlation. Is it possible that, when subjects are stressed, bright children give a better account of themselves than when the subjects are more neglected? Third, is the positive correlation between IQ and AR gain more likely to be higher in rural than in urban schools? In rural schools, more grades than one are usually working in the same room. This gives an opportunity for the brighter children to follow the work that is being done in classes ahead of their own. In urban schools this opportunity appears to be lacking.

DOES THE INITIAL AR OF THE CLASS AFFECT THE VALIDITY OF THE FORMULA FOR MEASURING TEACHING EFFICIENCY?

Another view commonly held is that any teacher is penalized by the formula for measuring his efficiency if he starts the work of the year with a class whose AR is already normal, and, conversely, a teacher is more likely to secure a high efficiency rating by the formula if the pupils with whom he starts have AR's below normal, *i.e.*, below 100.

This view has a variety of origins. Franzen contends, in opposition to the position taken by McCall, that it is impossible, except through inaccuracies of measurement, for a pupil to secure an AR above 100, interpreting an AR of 100 as always representing a pupil's utmost capacity. If Franzen's opinion is the correct one, it naturally is impossible for a pupil to do better than his best, and hence any teacher who starts with a class of pupils whose AR's are already up to or above 100 does not have the same possibilities for manifesting an improvement such as can be made by a teacher whose pupils' AR's can be increased.

A second origin of this view is in the frequently observed fact that when a pupil begins to reach high levels of any ability additional levels are more and more difficult to grow up to, particularly when gain is measured by means of unscaled tests. By analogy it is assumed that a like situation obtains in the case of growth in AR.

A third source of this view is again argument by analogy, this time from the realm of physics. When a pupil's AR is low, this means that his intellectual level is above his educational level. This gap is often thought of as a sort of vacuum which itself has power by a sort of suction to aid the pupil to lift his educational status more nearly to that of his intellectual status.

In order to determine the effect of the initial AR it was necessary to determine the correlation between initial AR and AR gain. In doing this the mean initial AR and the mean AR gain for each class could not be used, for the same reason that similar measures could not validly be used in determining the effect of initial IQ upon the validity of the teaching efficiency formula. Consequently, the correlation was found between pupil initial AR and pupil AR gain as was done in the study of the effect of IQ. Also as was done in studying the effect of IQ, the method of fused correlation was used and on the same pupils.

The correlations found for the subjects were as follows:

Initial reading A with reading AR gain	—.399
Initial arithmetic AR with arithmetic AR gain	—.109
Initial spelling AR with spelling AR gain	—.063
Initial composition AR with composition AR gain	—.374
Initial penmanship AR with penmanship AR gain	—.428

The foregoing correlations enable us to state the following conclusions for the groups studied, assuming that the technique standardized other factors:

1. Those pupils who start the year with high penmanship AR's will have more difficulty in increasing the size of their penmanship AR's than those pupils who start the year with lower penmanship AR's.

2. Those pupils who start the year with high reading AR's or high composition AR's are less likely to increase the size of their reading or composition AR's, respectively, than pupils who start the year with lower AR's in these subjects.

3. The same conclusions that have just been stated for penmanship, reading and composition also hold for spelling and arithmetic, but in less degree. Spelling in particular shows a negative r scarcely above zero.

Why this difference between arithmetic and spelling on the one hand and the other three subjects on the other? It will be recalled that the variability among the mean AR's are much greater for spelling, composition and penmanship than arithmetic and spelling. Inferences from this and from observations of actual AR gains for the individual pupils are that pupils also varied much more in reading, composition and penmanship than they did in arithmetic and spelling. Other things being equal, the greater the variability the greater the correlation. Hence the difference in variability probably explains some if not all of the difference found between the two groups of r's.

4. The foregoing conclusion makes it plausible, though, as said before, it does not make it certain, that what is true for pupils is likewise true for classes, namely, that any teacher is handicapped who is asked to teach a group of pupils whose AR's are high. The negative r's on which this conclusion is based are relatively small, so that practically they do not seriously invalidate the formula for measuring a teacher's efficiency. Even so they are large enough to be disturbing.

But before we accept the probability that we have found here evidence that the teaching efficiency formula is somewhat unfair to certain teachers, it is well to point out some compensating factors which tend to re-establish confidence in its justice.

It is very easy to fall into the error of thinking that the negative r's found between initial AR and AR gain are compensated by the disturbing, though lower, positive r's found between IQ and AR gain. But this does not constitute a compensating factor. These two sets of r's really tell about the same sort of story. Abundance of evidence collected by many investigators before this study was begun shows that high IQ's tend to have low AR's and low IQ's tend to have high AR's. Inspection of scatter diagrams based upon the data of this study confirms these earlier findings. The intricate interrelations of these three sets of facts will, we trust, be made clear by the following statements. High IQ's tend to make high AR gains. High IQ's tend to have low initial AR's. Low initial AR's tend to make high AR gains. Hence the disturbing effects of IQ and initial AR reinforce each other rather than balance each other.

It is not proposed to attempt an explanation of the apparent inconsistency of high IQ's making large AR gains and yet having lower AR's at the beginning of the year than low IQ pupils. It may be suggested in passing that these two facts are not necessarily inconsistent, for high IQ's may have received a different sort of treatment during the progress of this experiment from what they had been regularly receiving since they entered school.

What arguments can be brought forward, then, that will tend to re-establish confidence in the fairness of the formula for measuring teaching efficiency? There is a compensating factor, but it operates much more subtly than the two factors just considered to reinforce each other or reproduce each other through their mutual correlation. The writer proposes to show the invalidity of drawing similar inferences from apparently similar sets of r's.

It was inferred that because there is positive correlation between pupil IQ and pupil AR gain there is likely to be positive correlation between class mean IQ and class mean AR gain in case the teachers of the different classes are equal in teaching skill. The writer does not wish to dispute this inference but does desire to criticise sharply the assumption made in the fourth conclusion above that a like inference is as possible from r's based upon pupils to r's based upon means for classes. The ubiquitous errors in all mental measurements operate differently in the two situations.

Even though the formula for measuring teaching efficiency were utterly fair to teachers with classes of different initial AR, and even though the correlation were exactly zero between class mean initial AR and class mean AR gain for many teachers of exactly equal teaching skill, a negative r would still be found between initial AR and AR gain for the individual pupils within these classes. This follows inescapably from the fixation of growth in mental age from initial mental age to final mental age due to the fact that final mental age was computed from knowledge of initial mental age and IQ, instead of redetermining mental age again by means of a second intelligence test, and also from the manner in which erroneous initial reading ages, arithmetic ages, etc., readjusted themselves in the second testing of these abilities.

Imagine a pupil who, through a fortunate combination of errors of measurement, secured an initial mental age higher than the

CRITICISM OF THE EFFICIENCY FORMULA 85

truth, *i.e.*, higher than what would be his average from repeated measurements. Imagine also that his initial reading age was equally too high. This would yield an initial AR of 100. Now when it comes to the second testing, the final mental age will remain too high because it is not tested again but calculated from the initial mental age and IQ. The final reading age, on the contrary, will most probably not be as much above the true reading age as the final mental age is above the true mental age. The most probable thing is that it will be relatively lower. This is because there are more chances that errors of measurement the second time will operate to give the pupil a reading age nearer the truth than the first reading age. The effect of this would be to make the final AR less than the initial AR. The effect of this, in turn, would be to produce a minus reading AR change. Thus the net effect of a relatively high initial reading AR associated with a relatively low reading AR gain would be to create an appearance of negative correlation, provided always that the records of other pupils were operating differently. And that they would be operating differently will be shown next.

Imagine, again, that this pupil's initial mental age is too high, as in the first illustration. Imagine further that errors of measurement this time throw the initial reading age too low. This will make the initial reading AR lower than the truth. The final mental age will be too high also. The final reading age will most probably be relatively higher than the initial reading age, which will cause the final reading AR to be higher than the initial reading AR. The first illustration showed how initial high reading AR was associated with low reading AR gain, whereas this illustration shows how initial low reading AR is associated with final high reading AR gain. Thus both these situations produced by error are working toward negative correlation.

Other illustrations could be given for mental ages too high, just high enough and too low for the truth in combination with subject ages too high, just high enough and too low for the truth, together with the effects produced by these combinations upon initial AR, final AR and AR gains. It is only when the initial subject age is truth that the tendency will be for the correlation between initial AR and AR gain to be zero. All other initial combinations, according to the law of probability, will tend toward the production of negative correlations.

86 *EFFICIENCY IN SUPERVISION AND TEACHING*

This, in the judgment of the writer, explains most if not all of the negative r's found between initial AR and AR gain. So far as the negative r's are the results of errors of measurement as pointed out above, just so far they do not invalidate the formula for the measurement of teacher efficiency. It is here that a comforting compensation takes place. When the mean AR gains are computed for a class and hence for a teacher, the AR gains that are too high are balanced by the AR gains that are too low.

To sum up, there is good reason to believe that the negative r's found between initial AR and AR gain are not due to imperfection in the formula for measuring teaching efficiency so much as to errors of measurement and the effort that probability makes to correct these errors, and further that these errors can be present without invalidating the mean AR gain as a true measure of a teacher's efficiency.

DOES THE FORMULA FOR THE MEASUREMENT OF TEACHING EFFICIENCY YIELD A VALID MEASURE OF GENERAL TEACHING EFFICIENCY?

When this investigation of the efficiency of teachers was planned, it was hoped that one of the outcomes of the investigation would be proof that the application of the teacher efficiency formula to a few subjects would yield a series of measures for each teacher which, when averaged, would give a reasonably reliable, valid and adequate measure of that teacher. To what extent has this particular hope been realized?

Can valid measures of this efficiency be secured? Validity might be questioned on the grounds that there are no standard tests which measure genuine objectives of teaching. Such criticism will commend itself to all informed individuals as palpably unjustified. There are many standard tests which measure highly important outcomes of teaching.

Validity might be questioned in the second place on the ground that the formula favored teachers of pupils with high IQ's or low IQ's or pupils with high initial AR's or low initial AR's. This study has shown that these factors probably have little or no influence upon the validity of the formula.

Validity might be questioned in the third place on the ground that the formula is unsound because the AR upon which it depends is not valid, owing to the denominator in the AR formula being

CRITICISM OF THE EFFICIENCY FORMULA 87

composed of mental age only, which may not be the only determiner of AR possibilities. Perhaps certain aspects of purposing are sufficiently native and significant in terms of potentiality for educational growth to be in the denominator of the formula also. Again, it might be urged that intelligence status has little to do in determining the potentiality for progress in, say, penmanship. Both these criticisms may be true enough so far as individual pupils are concerned, though Franzen's [12] dissertation led him to conclude that they are not true; but perfect correlation between intelligence and potentiality is not required to give reasonable validity to the formula when mean scores for a whole class are being used.

Since the formula can meet reasonably well the criticism that it is unreliable and not valid, this brings us to the question as to the extent to which we can depend upon it to give a measure of a teacher's general efficiency. Here the prospect is rather discouraging.

The prospect is discouraging because the validity that has been claimed for the formula is claimed only for such functions as reading, arithmetic, history as a body of facts and principles, and geography. This claim is restricted to the skill and intellectual aspects of education because we are almost totally lacking in information as to the validity of the AR formula in the realm of purposes, attitudes, ideals, and the like. We are extremely ignorant as to the extent to which intelligence is an index of the pupil's possibilities for making progress in acquiring these aspects of education. It may be that dull children submit themselves more readily to our attempts to inculcate purposes than do their brighter classmates. All must have noticed the distinct tendency for bright children to be radical in the sense that they consider purposes to be the peculiarly personal and private concern of the pupil himself. Until this realm is brought under the teacher efficiency formula, a general efficiency measure for a teacher cannot be determined, for most educators are in agreement that the teaching of purposes is a vital part of a teacher's work.

There is one gleam of immediate promise, however. There is some ground for believing that teachers who are most skillful in teaching intellectual abilities are likewise most skillful in teaching purposes. This contention has a double foundation. One is that positive correlation is usually found between desirable traits.

Another is that the effort put forth by a child in studying reading, arithmetic, history and the like is a direct index of how successful the teacher has been in inculcating right purposes and right methods of work. It is probable that the most effective way for a teacher to go about developing reading, arithmetic and such subjects is first of all to give attention to purposes and methods of work. If this should prove to be true we can probably dismiss our fears that the effect of measuring teacher efficiency by means of even the standard tests now available will be to distract attention from what many educators consider more vital matters. Whether or not it is true can in the judgment of the writer be determined readily in the near future.

If we accept this conclusion on faith for the present, we come to the final question as to whether it is feasible to secure a measure of general teaching efficiency in the realm of abilities only. The researches of Franzen plus the critical evaluations of this chapter make it possible to conclude that it is feasible to secure such a measure of a teacher's efficiency.

Unfortunately, this investigation also shows that, while such a measure is feasible, the process of securing it will be rather a laborious one to follow. It was hoped that the average of a teacher's efficiency in teaching a few fundamental subjects would give a satisfactory index of his general efficiency in teaching all such subjects. The extremely low coefficients of correlation, reported in preceding chapters, between teachers' efficiency in teaching one subject and their efficiency in teaching any other subject mean that efficiency in many subjects must be measured and combined before it is safe to assume that the average so secured is a fairly accurate index of what the average would be if a great many or all subjects were similarly measured. It is not possible to assume with much assurance that if a teacher is efficient in teaching reading he will be efficient in teaching arithmetic or composition.

How many subjects must be measured before confidence can be placed in the composite? One way to answer this important practical question is to combine the results from any two subjects and correlate the composite so formed with a composite of every possible pair of the other subjects. If the resulting correlations prove too low for practical purposes, then any three can be combined and correlated with any other three. This process can be continued until the correlations become high enough to be satisfactory.

This study shows that an efficiency measure in one subject is not an adequate basis for practical use except within that subject. It does not permit us to predict with assurance success with all subjects. Scatter diagrams were constructed to show the amount of correlation between various pairs of subjects and various other pairs. Inspection of these scatter diagrams showed that the correlations were thereby raised, but even so they were still far below what is required for practical purposes of "hiring and firing" and demoting and promoting teachers. Unfortunately, not enough subjects were measured in this study to enable this process to be continued beyond that of pairing. Consequently, resort must be had to some other method of securing an estimate of the number of subjects that need to be measured to secure an approximately accurate measure of general teaching efficiency.

It might be contended that the subjects measured in this study are random samples of all the subjects that the teacher teaches, in the same sense that a second duplicate test is a random sampling of the same ability that was first tested. This would seem to justify the use of the Spearman-Brown prophecy formula in order to determine the number of subjects that would have to be measured. The analogy is far from perfect, so that the use of the prophecy formula for this purpose would yield a very crude estimate indeed. Nevertheless, there appears to be no other alternative, except to attempt no estimate at all. With this caution the publication below of the results yielded by this formula can do no harm, and they are worthy of some attention.

The Spearman-Brown prophecy formula in the form given in McCall's [13] *How to Experiment in Education* is:

$$rx = \frac{Nr_1}{1 + (N-1)r_1}$$

Where rx is the size of the coefficient of correlation desired for practical purposes, r_1 is the r between one subject and another, or, in our situation, the mean of the r's between each subject and all the other subjects for both rural and urban teachers.

The mean of all the intercorrelations for all subjects for both rural and urban schools is .16. If we set .8 as the lowest correlation that is at all acceptable for practical use, and substitute this for rx in the formula, while we substitute .16 for r_1 in the formula, and then if we solve for N, the answer becomes 21. This means that twenty-one subjects, or better, twenty-one different aspects of subjects, must be measured and the results averaged before an index of general teaching efficiency suitable for practical use can be secured. Since it may appear doubtful to some whether there are twenty-one subjects in the curriculum, the best way to summarize the foregoing is to say that evidence to date indicates that teachers must be measured in practically every subject before we are in a position to know with assurance what their general efficiency is.

The situation is possibly not quite so bad as this. It is probable that we have a right to use a coefficient of correlation for r_1 in the foregoing formula that is higher than .16. There is probably present in all the data used in this study a subtle see-saw factor operating to produce lower correlations than the true correlations. Imagine two teachers of equal training and natural talent for teaching. One decides to emphasize reading, which inevitably means that penmanship, say, will be somewhat neglected, while the other decides to emphasize penmanship, which means that reading will be somewhat neglected. The effect of this dependence of one subject upon the emphasis given to another subject or other subjects is to produce a negative correlation or a lower positive correlation than the true correlation between any two subjects.

The words "true correlation" are used here in a special sense. They mean the correlation that it is possible to secure between the efficiency measures for these two teachers, had both elected to give the same emphasis to the two subjects of reading and penmanship. Since the teachers were teaching several subjects instead of just two, the distribution of emphasis becomes too bewildering to be corrected by conventional statistical procedures. In proportion as more and more subjects are combined into a composite efficiency measure for a teacher, these see-saw effects which are "cutting the throat" of intercorrelations between separate subjects have their influence minimized. If this hypothesis is a true one, the estimate that twenty-one subject aspects must be measured in order to secure an adequate measure of a teacher's general efficiency is excessive. If the see-saw effect is genuine, the writer knows no way to eliminate its baleful influence except to increase the number of subjects measured, and then proceed by empirical combinations of these to determine just how many subjects need to be tested in order to secure a satisfactory index of general teaching efficiency.

PART THREE

CHAPTER IX

SUMMARY AND CONCLUSIONS

This study is divided into two main divisions. Part I describes a practical program of supervision based upon intelligence and educational tests, and attempts an evaluation of the worth of such a program.

Part II summarizes the stages in the evolution of methods for the measurement of a teacher's efficiency, and then describes the results secured from the application of the latest technique to a group of urban and rural teachers. The data, so secured, were used to answer many questions as to the amount of relationship that exists between ability to teach certain subjects and certain other subjects, between ability to teach a subject and supervisors' estimate of teacher's ability to teach that same subject, between ability to teach skills and supervisors' estimate of ability to teach character and everything except character, between professional knowledge and ability to teach, and the like.

Part II closes with a critical study of the validity of the formula for measuring teachers' efficiency. Here an attempt is made to determine to what extent, if at all, the validity of the formula is conditioned by the type of school in which a teacher teaches, the initial Intelligence Quotient of the class and the initial Accomplishment Ratio of the class.

A more detailed summary of Part I and Part II follows:

1. The supervision phase of this study took place in a residential town with a population of about 10,000, situated on the outskirts of a large city.

2. A testing program was undertaken in grades three to eight inclusive by a director of measurement in order to answer certain questions formulated by the superintendent and principals. Detailed

advice about the organization and administration of such a program is given.

3. Tests of intelligence, reading, arithmetic, spelling, composition and penmanship were applied according to the standard procedure, and crude scores for the pupils were converted into mental ages, reading ages, etc.

4. The abilities that were measured first in October, 1922, were measured again in October, 1923.

5. The program of testing was followed by a program of supervision, the first step of which was to report the results secured from the tests at a general meeting of the entire teaching and supervisory staff. Here results were brought to bear upon the questions concerning each of the separate schools as a whole.

6. The second step was to bring the results to bear upon the separate classes and individual pupils in these classes. This was accomplished in teachers' meetings within each school concerned. Matters discussed at these meetings were: degree of attainment of age, grade and intelligence norms, regulation of educational emphasis, reclassification of pupils, and the like.

7. Other phases of the supervision program included lectures by the director of measurement to parent-teachers' association meetings, reports to the board of education, testing for the formation of special classes, parent interviews, improvement of teachers' examinations, etc.

8. An enumeration was made of errors to be avoided in the planning and administration of a program of supervision based on measurement.

9. A technique was evolved for evaluating the foregoing program. The description of this technique is followed by a critical discussion of it.

10. This technique was applied and the educational value of the program determined.

11. Part II begins with a summary of the stages in the evolution of a valid method of measuring the efficiency of teachers. These are, in temporal order: general impression stage, score card and human ladder stage, and objective measurement stage. The merits and defects of each type are pointed out, thus justifying the selection of the Accomplishment Ratio teaching efficiency formula for use in this study.

12. The data for each teacher to which the Accomplishment

SUMMARY AND CONCLUSIONS 93

Ratio teaching efficiency formula was applied were the results from the initial and final tests in the urban schools, and a like set of initial and final tests in the rural schools in Queen Anne's County, Maryland. The interval between the initial and final testing in the rural schools was six months.

13. Queen Anne's County has the usual types of rural school, namely, one-room, two-room, and three-or-more-than-three room.

14. The computation of an efficiency measure in, say, reading for each teacher in either rural or urban situation involved the computation of initial mental age, initial reading age, initial Reading Accomplishment Ratio, Intelligence Quotient, final mental age, final reading age, final Reading Accomplishment Ratio, gain or loss in Reading Accomplishment Ratio, and mean gain or loss for the class. This last gave the teacher's efficiency in teaching reading. By a similar process mean Accomplishment changes were computed for arithmetic, spelling, composition, and penmanship.

15. Judgments were secured from presumably competent judges as to the relative worth of a gain in reading as compared with a gain in each of the other subjects. Using these as weights, the mean Accomplishment Ratio changes for the different subjects were weighted, through knowledge of their variability, and combined to form a composite measure of teaching efficiency as determined by means of objective tests.

16. The Standard Deviation of the means for all the teachers for each subject was 8.3 for reading, 4.2 for arithmetic, 2.9 for spelling, 7.7 for composition, and 7.4 for penmanship.

17. The product-moment coefficient of correlation was computed between reading efficiency measures and efficiency measures for each of the other subjects. The mean of these four correlations of r's is .13 for the rural and .26 for the urban teachers.

18. The mean of the r's between arithmetic and the other four subjects is .10 for the rural and .26 for the urban teachers.

19. The mean of the r's between spelling and the other four subjects is .10 for the rural and .14 for the urban teachers.

20. The mean of the r's between composition and the other four subjects is .20 for the rural and .17 for the urban teachers.

21. The mean of the r's between penmanship and the other four subjects is .00 for the rural and .25 for the urban teachers.

22. In the rural schools there is a general tendency for efficient teachers of penmanship to be inefficient teachers of reading, arith-

metic and spelling. This tendency was not found for the urban teachers.

23. There is a general tendency for intercorrelations between objective efficiency measures to be higher for urban teachers than for rural teachers. This greater regularity for urban schools would probably be expected by all.

24. The three highest correlations were in order: .46 (urban) between arithmetic and penmanship, .43 (urban) between reading and arithmetic, and .32 (rural) between composition and penmanship.

25. The three most negative correlations were in order: −.19 (rural) between spelling and penmanship, −.11 (rural) between reading and penmanship, and −.01 (rural) between arithmetic and penmanship.

26. The three lowest correlations were in order: −.01 (rural) between arithmetic and penmanship, .06 (urban) between arithmetic and composition, and .07 (rural) between arithmetic and composition.

27. In general, a teacher's ability to teach a narrow skill can be predicted more accurately from knowledge of his ability to teach a wider skill than from knowledge of his ability to teach another narrow skill.

28. In general, a teacher's ability to teach a wider skill can be predicted more accurately from knowledge of his ability to teach another like type of skill than from knowledge of his ability to teach a narrow skill.

29. A teacher's ability to teach a wider skill can be predicted from knowledge of his ability to teach a like type of skill more accurately than his ability to teach a narrow skill can be predicted from knowledge of his ability to teach another narrow skill.

30. Urban teachers were ranked by one supervisor on three qualities, namely, ability to teach reading, ability to teach everything except character and ability to teach character. The rural teachers were ranked on the same qualities by three supervisors in conference.

31. These supervisory estimates were correlated with objective measures of teacher efficiency.

32. The r between ability to teach reading and supervisory estimate of that ability is .27 for rural and −.36 for urban teachers.

33. The r between composite objective efficiency and supervisory

SUMMARY AND CONCLUSIONS 95

estimate of ability to teach everything except character is .33 for rural and −.25 for urban teachers.

34. The r between composite objective efficiency and supervisory estimate of ability to build character is .32 for rural and −.12 for urban teachers.

35. The r between composite objective efficiency and supervisory estimate of ability to teach in general is .32 for rural and −.26 for urban teachers.

36. There is a very high intercorrelation between the three joint rankings given the rural teachers by the three supervisors. The r's are .9906, .98893 and .98894. The mean of similar rankings of seven other supervisors in different situations gave r's of .8843, .7815 and .8057.

37. Approximately 100 graduate students in education made guesses as to what the foregoing correlations would turn out to be.

38. Among these judges, there was great divergence of opinion as to what the correlations would be found to be.

39. There were especially wide divergences of opinion as to the amount of correlation that would be found to exist between composite objective efficiency and supervisory rankings on ability to build character, between ability to teach reading and supervisory estimate of this ability, and between ability to teach reading and ability to teach penmanship.

40. There was a strong tendency to overestimate the size of the r's actually found. In estimating the absolute size of the r's the judges went wide of the mark, but they were surprisingly accurate in estimating relative size.

41. The rural teachers were tested with the Steele-Herring test of professional knowledge and the scores made were correlated with composite objective efficiency scores. The r is .046. This indicates that there is no correlation between how much teachers know about modern educational ideas and practices as measured by the Steele-Herring test and how well they teach.

42. The r between professional knowledge and ranking by supervisors for general teaching ability is .407.

43. A distribution was made of the class mean AR changes by subjects and types of schools.

44. In general the largest amount of AR change is in reading and penmanship. The smallest is in spelling. All subjects show more than normal AR gain.

45. The AR changes are extremely variable in reading, composition and penmanship. Spelling shows the least variability.

46. The AR progress in urban schools was much less than in the rural schools.

47. In general three-room schools made more progress than two-room schools and two-room schools made more progress than one-room schools.

48. The largest amount of progress in penmanship and spelling was made by one-room and two-room schools respectively.

49. It is impossible with the data of this study to determine whether the type of school affects the validity of the teacher efficiency formula.

50. The Intelligence Quotients for one-room, two-room and three-room schools are 93.8, 94.5 and 103.6, respectively.

51. The teacher-efficiency formula penalizes the teacher with high IQ pupils, provided these pupils also have high mental ages.

52. A fused correlation method was developed in order to facilitate the computation of the r between IQ and AR changes within each class. The fused r is .197 between IQ and reading AR change, .017 between IQ and arithmetic AR change, $-.046$ between IQ and spelling AR change, .042 between IQ and composition AR change, and .126 between IQ and penmanship AR change. From these r's, it may be tentatively inferred that IQ of pupils affects only very slightly the validity of the teacher-efficiency formula. Contrary to conventional opinion, the teacher of bright pupils is benefited unless these pupils have high mental ages.

53. The fused r was computed between initial AR of pupils in each subject within each class and AR changes in that subject. The r's are $-.399$ for reading, $-.109$ for arithmetic, $-.063$ for spelling, $-.374$ for composition and $-.428$ for penmanship. It is shown that errors of measurement plus the assumption of constancy of IQ are responsible for some, if not all, of this negative correlation, thus justifying a tentative conclusion that initial AR of pupils does not affect the validity of the teacher-efficiency formula.

54. Part II closes with a discussion of the extent to which the teacher efficiency formula yields a reliable and valid measure of general teaching efficiency.

55. Assuming the data of this study to be representative, the chief conclusions of Part II are:

SUMMARY AND CONCLUSIONS

a. Teaching efficiency cannot be judged by supervisors accurately enough to be of any practical value.

b. Teaching efficiency cannot be determined by testing a teacher's knowledge of modern educational ideas and practices.

c. Teaching efficiency in special fields can be measured accurately by means of the teaching efficiency formula without making much, if any, allowance for pupils' IQ's or initial AR's.

d. This study shows that many aspects of teaching must be measured by the teacher efficiency formula before a sufficiently accurate measure of teacher efficiency for practical purposes can be secured.

REFERENCES AND BIBLIOGRAPHY

1. W. A. McCALL. *How to Measure in Education.* New York: Macmillan Company.
2. HERRING AND WILNER. *Manual for Measuring a School.* Yonkers-on-Hudson, New York: World Book Company.
3. CALDWELL AND COURTIS. *Then and Now in Education.* New York: The Macmillan Company.
4. E. C. ELLIOTT. "How Shall the Merit of Teachers Be Tested and Recorded?" *Educational Administration and Supervision,* 1:291-99 (May 1915).
5. NEW YORK BUREAU OF MUNICIPAL RESEARCH. *Score Card.* New York City.
6. H. O. RUGG. *A Rating Scale for Judging Teachers in Service.* Chicago, Illinois: University of Chicago.
7. R. FRANZEN. "The Accomplishment Quotient." *Teachers College Record,* 21:432 (November, 1920).
8. W. S. MONROE AND B. R. BUCKINGHAM. *The Illinois Examination, I and II, The Teacher's Handbook.* Bloomington, Illinois: The Public School Publishing Company.
9. T. L. KELLEY. *Statistical Method.* New York: The Macmillan Company.
10. E. M. BAILOR. *Content and Form in Tests of Intelligence.* New York: Teachers College, Columbia University.
11. P. B. KNIGHT. *Qualities Related to Success in Teaching.* New York: Teachers College, Columbia University.
12. R. FRANZEN. *The Accomplishment Ratio.* New York: Teachers College, Columbia University.
13. W. A. McCALL. *How to Experiment in Education.* New York: Macmillan Company.

NOTE: For a more comprehensive annotated bibliography see W. S. Monroe and John A. Clark; *Measuring Teaching Efficiency. University of Illinois Bulletin;* University of Illinois, Urbana, Illinois.